What's a Parent to Do?

New Frontiers in Education
Edited by Dr. Frederick M. Hess

This Rowman & Littlefield series provides educational leaders, entrepreneurs, and researchers the opportunity to offer insights that stretch the boundaries of thinking on education. Educational entrepreneurs and leaders have too rarely shared their experiences and insights. Research has too often been characterized by impenetrable jargon. This series aims to foster volumes that can inform, educate, and inspire aspiring reformers and allow them to learn from the trials of some of today's most dynamic doers; provide researchers with a platform for explaining their work in language that allows policymakers and practitioners to take full advantage of its insights; and establish a launch pad for fresh ideas and hard-won experience. Whether an author is a prominent leader in education, a researcher, or an entrepreneur, the key criterion for inclusion in *New Frontiers in Education* is a willingness to challenge conventional wisdom and pat answers. The series editor, Frederick M. Hess, is the director of education policy studies at the American Enterprise Institute and can be reached at rhess@aei.org or (202) 828–6030.

Titles in Series

Choosing Excellence in Public Schools: Where There's a Will, There's a Way, David W. Hornbeck and Katherine Conner (2009)

It's the Classroom, Stupid: A Plan to Save America's Schoolchildren, Kalman R. Hettleman (2010)

Social Entrepreneurship in Education: Private Ventures for the Public Good, Michael R. Sandler (2010)

Standing and Delivering: What the Movie Didn't Tell, Henry Gradillas and Jerry Jesness (2010)

Taking Measure of Charter Schools: Better Assessments, Better Policymaking, Better Schools, Julian R. Betts and Paul T. Hill (2010)

Working for Kids: Educational Leadership as Inquiry and Invention, James H. Lytle (2010)

From Family Collapse to America's Decline: The Educational, Economic, and Social Costs of Family Fragmentation, Mitch Pearlstein (2011)

Teaching America: The Case for Civic Education, David J. Feith (2011)

The Urban School System of the Future: Applying the Principles and Lessons of Chartering, Andy Smarick (2012)

Blueprint for School System Transformation: A Vision for Comprehensive Reform in Milwaukee and Beyond, Frederick Hess and Carolyn Sattin- Bajaj (2013)

Breaking the Cycle: How Schools Can Overcome Urban Challenges, Nancy Brown Diggs (2013)

Trendsetting Charter Schools: Raising the Bar for Civic Education, Gary J. Schmitt and Cheryl Miller (2015)

What's A Parent to Do?: How to Help Your Child Select the Right College, Anne D. Neal (2017)

What's a Parent to Do?

How to Help Your Child Select the Right College

Anne D. Neal

ROWMAN & LITTLEFIELD
London · New York

Published by Rowman & Littlefield
A wholly owned subsidiary of The Rowman & Littlefield Publishing Group, Inc.
4501 Forbes Boulevard, Suite 200, Lanham, Maryland 20706
www.rowman.com

Unit A, Whitacre Mews, 26-34 Stannary Street, London SE11 4AB

British Library Cataloguing in Publication Information Available

Library of Congress Cataloging-in-Publication Data

978-1-4758-0881-0 (cloth : alk. paper)
978-1-4758-0882-7 (pbk. : alk. paper)
978-1-4758-0883-4 (electronic)

∞™ The paper used in this publication meets the minimum requirements of American National Standard for Information Sciences—Permanence of Paper for Printed Library Materials, ANSI/NISO Z39.48–1992.

Printed in the United States of America

Contents

Foreword   vii

Preface   ix

ZEROING IN ON YOUR SCHOOLS   **1**

1   Brace Yourself   3

2   Make a Match   7

DOING RESEARCH   **19**

3   Insist on Academic Substance   21

4   Look for Serious and Responsible Teaching   33

5   Understand Dorm Life   41

6   Get the Facts on Drinking, Socializing, and Campus Culture   47

7   Put a Premium on Free Speech   51

8   Aim for Four Years and Out   57

9   Learn the Real Cost   63
    Dr. Richard Vedder, distinguished professor of economics
    emeritus, Ohio University

10 Visit with Your Eyes Open   73

REMAINING INVOLVED   **77**

11 Stay Connected   79

12   Conclusion: Jump Right In!   87

Postscript: Take Action   89

Acknowledgments   91

Selecting a College Checklist   93

Appendix A: Share This Letter. Advice to College Freshmen   95

Appendix B: Model Legislation   97

Notes   103

About the Author   125

Foreword

There is no American *system* of higher education. Colleges and universities are abundant and varied, from enormous state institutions to tiny Christian colleges, from two-year art colleges to universities offering undergraduate, postgraduate, and professional degrees in multiple combinations and in every subject under the sun.

It's a free market—but one with more than a few oddities and even some minefields. There is no consensus about what should count as "quality" and "value," or how to measure them. Nonetheless, as in any free market, those with the most information are in the best position to make good choices.

It's hard to know what to look for, and hard to know whether you've found it. This book will help you evaluate the providers of higher education.

Most colleges and universities are public charities even though they charge high prices for their services. But somewhere deep in the DNA of every not-for-profit college and university is a ghostly trace of its charitable and civic roots. Colleges and universities pay at least lip service—and in some cases, much more than that—to the idea that the public good and the development of wise and principled graduates are at the essence of their ancestry and purpose.

Yet, when not-for-profit colleges and universities compete for customers, their marketing efforts collide jarringly with their aspirations for social and moral purpose. A wise parent or prospective student will read between the lines to figure out what isn't being said. Beneath the boast "Ten swimming pools, and a rock climbing wall" may lurk the reality "Our gymnasium is more challenging than most of our courses!" And the picture of our diverse student body? It could well be digitally edited to get them together in one place!

This book will help you pry the truth out from the imagery. It will help you ask the right questions and it will make you think about what you want to do with the answers, which are rarely simply "right" or "wrong." It will point you to other reliable sources of information.

More than anything, *What's a Parent to Do?* will make you healthily skeptical without being cynical. Though sanctimony is commonplace in higher education, genuine piety is there too, if you know how to look for it.

Good luck on your search for a great education!

Harry R. Lewis
Gordon McKay Professor of Computer Science
Former Dean of Harvard College and Interim Dean
of the Harvard John A. Paulson School of
Engineering and Applied Sciences

Preface

WHAT'S A PARENT TO DO?

That's certainly a question I asked myself in the course of my daughter's college-application process.

And I know I am not alone. I've spent more than two decades in higher education, first at the National Endowment for the Humanities and then at the American Council of Trustees and Alumni, working with alumni and trustees around the country to improve higher education. And in those years I've seen many changes—including those that make the college-selection process more fraught than ever.

Each year, well over a million newly minted high school graduates enroll in colleges and universities across the country.[1] They—and their families—find themselves in the midst of an often lengthy, and almost always stressful exercise. A cottage industry of test prep companies, tutors, college advisors, and even psychiatrists has arisen to deal with the anxiety and emotions of vulnerable adolescents and (yes!) helicopter parents.[2]

For decades, parents and students assumed that all the stress and anxiety were worth the payoff. A college degree was a guarantee of a good job. It was part of growing up, a way of making contacts, and even meeting a spouse. Getting a college degree was the essence of the American dream.

Those assumptions are changing. In the past few years, there has been troubling news of declining standards, political correctness, and spiraling costs. Tuition sticker prices have gone up over 570 percent since 1982, and to no one's surprise, student debt has risen as well.[3] Student loan debt now outweighs credit card debt, and the stories of college graduates without jobs and living with their parents are rampant.[4]

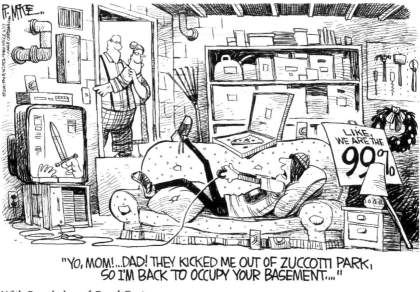

"YO, MOM!...DAD! THEY KICKED ME OUT OF ZUCCOTTI PARK, SO I'M BACK TO OCCUPY YOUR BASEMENT...."

With Permission of Cagel Cartoons.

Even though we spend on higher education substantially more than the per-student average of industrialized countries,[5] studies abound showing that too many colleges are offering little more than four, five, or six years of partying—and a big bill to show for it.[6] When surveyed, students themselves admit that a majority of their time in college is dedicated to sleeping and socializing, not studying. And after graduating, they are the first to lament the things they missed: a core curriculum, a common conversation asking—and answering—life's big questions, not to mention preparing for a meaningful career.[7]

Survey after survey shows that there is a wage premium for students who graduate from college. Those who attend only high school, on average, cannot expect to see the same salaries that a college graduate can see.[8] But across the country, policymakers and taxpayers—to say nothing of parents—are raising valid questions about the value of a college degree. And parents are wondering: What can I do to help my child choose a college that represents good value and a good fit?

In the next few chapters, we aim to address that question.

It's true: There is no single way to pick a college and no single reason for selecting one of over 3,000 four-year colleges and universities in America.[9] For some families, the selection process is an easy one—focused on the school closest to home. For others, it involves an elaborate review

---

Employers' View of Four-Year College Graduates

- **23.9%** find graduates' overall preparation "excellent."

- **64.5%** say "adequate."

- **26.2%** find their writing skills "deficient."

Source: **Linda Barrington and Jill Casner-Lotto, *Are They Really Ready to Work? Employers' Perspective on the Basic Knowledge and Applied Skills of New Entrants to the 21st Century U.S. Workforce* (The Conference Board, Corporate Voices for Working Families, The Partnership for 21st Century Skills, and the Society for Human Resource Management, 2006).**

of institutions, large and small, near and far, on the quest for the "perfect" choice. For others, it's pursuing institutions with a "reputation" and the social networks that have frequently proven even more valuable to graduates than what goes on in the classroom.

Whether your child attends a school next door or travels across the country, there are certain basic things that you can and should explore as you enter the college application process. Observations from family, friends, guidance counselors, and colleges are all fine and good, but any decision of this magnitude should also be grounded on real data. None of us should "fly blind" when facing this big decision or, worse, simply rely on a school's "reputation."

It is often hard to understand what to look at—even where to start. There are so many websites, so many marketing materials, and so many ideas—in the press, from guidance counselors, and from friends who have already been through the college-selection process.

This book is designed to be a guide. It provides chapters on curricula and teaching, dorm life, freedom of thought and speech, substance abuse, affordability, and more—issues that are very much in the news. It offers ways to gain insights into, and to ask questions about, these important matters before making a choice. And remember that at the end of the day, it's more often what students do, not where they go, that makes the difference. In a 2013 Gallup and Lumina Foundation poll, more than half of employers surveyed notably said they did not care where students obtained their degrees.[10]

Despite its immense budgets and oversized impact, higher ed still remains amazingly opaque, particularly when it comes to parents' knowing whether colleges and universities are really doing a good job.

By asking probing questions, parents—and, by extension, taxpayers and policymakers—can help move colleges and universities to greater transparency and greater results for our children. What's a parent to do?

Let's answer this question together.

Anne D. Neal
Washington, DC

ZEROING IN ON YOUR SCHOOLS

Chapter 1

Brace Yourself

Many of us remember the "good old days" when we went to university. But, in fact, nostalgia isn't what it used to be. Much has changed!

In 1990, the average annual bill for tuition and room and board in a public university in current dollars was $9,030; in a private, $24,049:[1] Students enrolled full-time and graduated in four years. And the majority of full-time students were ages eighteen to twenty-one.[2]

Today, the majority of the college-going population is nontraditional: That means that many are "adult learners," and nearly 40 percent of students attend part-time, going to college at night, on weekends, and often online, rather than having a residential college experience. Nearly 60 percent end up attending more than one school.[3]

Today, the average bill for tuition and room and board at public colleges around the country is $19,548 per year. At private colleges: $43,921.[4]

Tuitions have exploded and student-loan debt is now significantly higher than average credit card debt.[5]

What most people remember as a four-year commitment has now often become a five-year, six-year, or even longer experience—with added time raising total costs.[6]

And outcomes aren't always what they should be. A majority of surveyed employers recently lamented that they could not find college graduates with the skills and knowledge needed to compete in the global marketplace.[7] Sociologists Richard Arum and Josipa Roksa found that, across a range of schools, nearly 50 percent of students could show no significant gains in their skills over their first two years of college and 36 percent no significant gains after four—generally expensive—years![8]

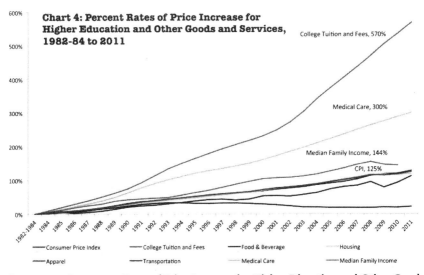

Figure 1.1. Percentage Rates of Price Increase for Higher Education and Other Goods and Services, 1982–1984 to 2011. *Source:* Bureau of Labor Statistics, Consumer Price Index (All Urban Consumers); other data from U.S. Census Bureau, Current Population Survey Annual Social and Economic Supplements, and American Community Survey.

Many graduates who are employed are postponing getting married, buying a home, and making life's larger decisions because they are so deeply in debt.[9]

Sadly, many states across the country are upping their tuitions and slashing financial aid. Access is shrinking, and that makes it even harder to have an honest reckoning about finances.

Presidents of public universities once proudly defended the role of their institutions to provide their states with an educated citizenry and a skilled workforce. Yet many of them have abandoned this special mission and advocate what amounts to privatization of public universities, especially flagship schools.[10] They raise tuitions to private-university levels and promise that in-state students will have access to increased financial aid.

There are serious flaws in this high tuition/high aid model, since the promise of increased financial aid for able, in-state students does not always materialize: Many tuition increases are not used for financial or grant aid, but simply raise the net price of attendance.[11] Families who once looked to affordable higher education as a ticket to a better life are now faced with crushing debt. This trend is a bad one. Schools have other ways of addressing budget shortfalls than privatization or higher levels of public appropriations.

Minimal Student Learning Gains

45% showed minimal to no improvement in two years.

36% showed minimal to no improvement in four years.

Richard Arum and Josipa Roksa, *Academically Adrift*. Limited Learning on College Campuses (Chicago: University of Chicago Press, 2011)

Figure 1.2. Minimal Student Learning Gains.

These trends in public higher education are one reason why income disparity is growing in our country. While institutional aid is widely available to low-income students, and the most affluent families can pay their own way, middle-class families often find themselves squeezed, left with limited financial aid and faced with the need to take out substantial personal loans, assuming considerable debt.[12]

In too many places, it is possible for students and families to invest a quarter million dollars in education—with little to show for it.

So what's a parent to do?

For starters, do as much research as you can. Use the check list in this book to make sure you are focusing on the most important information. Given the price you will pay, your child's college decision deserves truly thoughtful scrutiny. Every college has a website, and many send out reams of material to impress students and their families. Read it all.

You'll also want to know about the financial stability of the institution, particularly if you are looking at a small private college without an endowment. Higher education expert Jeffrey Selingo reports that: "One-third of all colleges and universities in the United States face financial statements significantly weaker than before the recession, and according to one analysis, are on an unsustainable fiscal path."[13]

You can gain insights through Moody's, which examines and rates the finances of more than 500 colleges and universities that issue bonds through public markets. *Forbes* magazine has provided good information on the financial stability of colleges around the country.[14]

There are also a vast number of college rankings, from the well-known *U.S. News & World Report* and the *Princeton Review* to the less-well-known but popular student guides on drinking and hooking up. But don't stop there. Most existing rankings focus on inputs and resources rather than what students take away when they leave. There's an old joke along these lines—Top schools are so rich because students bring so much and leave with so little. Regrettably, for some it's no joke.

SUMMING UP

Sure, reputation is important, but not at the expense of real learning and hard-earned resources. We'll deal with admission to "elite" schools, but I hope you will agree with me: What really matters is putting education ahead of reputation. Schools paint a shiny image—understandably! But the purpose of this book is to get past the image and down to the real nuts and bolts of the experience that your child will have and that you will finance.

Chapter 2

Make a Match

WHAT ARE YOU AND YOUR CHILD LOOKING FOR?

What is the college experience you are aiming for? Are you aiming for your child to develop specific job skills within a career path; to become a thoughtful person capable of critical thinking and negotiating his or her own way through life; or to have an opportunity for athletic development aimed at a professional career?

How you answer this question will determine some of the choices you make and the schools you examine. For starters, "colleges" typically are smaller institutions, focused exclusively on undergraduates. "Universities" are generally larger, with both undergraduate and graduate programs. Not all colleges and universities are good at the same things.[1]

ACADEMIC EXPECTATIONS?

To help answer basic questions for any given school, start by finding a college's mission statement. Does it set valid educational goals? Or does it sound more like a community action project? And find graduation requirements. Do they reflect a serious conception of what every educated person should know? Are requirements outside the major met by a selection of coherent, comprehensive, and well-planned courses or by a grab bag of dozens of unrelated courses?

AND THEN, ANSWER THESE!

City vs. Country

Location, of course, can make a difference. There is much to be found in a big city—at the campus and outside of it: access to celebrity speakers, proximity to cultural and athletic events, and more. By comparison, more rural campuses may not have the same volume of activity. Tales abound of students "in the middle of nowhere" who seek excitement off campus. Road trip!

But a country school and an invigorating campus life are not mutually exclusive. Take a look at Sewanee—The University of the South. Located on a mountaintop roughly fifty miles from any big city or other educational institution,[2] this campus has achieved a wonderful balance of seriousness and fun; parties, yes, but rigorous academics too.[3]

If you and your child have grown up in a big city, would trying a rural college be fun—or would it be too different from the busy city life you know? This is a decision that only you can make.

At the end of the day, it's important to remember: college shouldn't be a playground if it is truly going to be meaningful. Picking a school should ultimately be based on issues of educational quality.

In-State or Out?

Research shows that most students attend schools within easy driving distance from their home. According to the Department of Education, 81 percent of undergraduates in 2012 were enrolled in schools less than 100 miles from their backyard. A mere 8 percent were enrolled in schools more than 500 miles away.[4]

The option of living at home and the lower tuitions generally available to students in-state make this an appealing option. But here again, things are changing. In recent years, many public institutions have been raising their pricing for in-state tuition and fees—some, as in the University of California system after the 2008 recession, by as much as 60 percent.[5]

Increasingly, administrators also look to foreign and out-of-state students—who pay much higher tuition rates—to balance the books. At the University of Oregon, the number of in-state students declined from 70.4 percent in fall 2004 to 51.2 percent in fall 2015. At the University of Alabama in fall 2014, a mere 36 percent of freshmen were in-state.[6] That means that it's harder and harder for many in-state students to get into the public colleges or universities of their choice.

Ironically, it now often costs less for a student to attend a "pricey" Ivy League school than it does to attend one of the national public universities. Harvard, for example, boasts on its website that "for more than 90 percent of

American and international families, Harvard costs the same or less than the U.S. public universities." Harvard requires no contribution from families with annual incomes below $65,000 and asks for 10 percent of income or less from families earning between $65,000 and $150,000.

Even families with incomes greater than $150,000 can be eligible for aid at a number of colleges, depending on particular circumstances, such as multiple children in college or unusual medical or other essential expenses.[7]

Large vs. Small?

Large schools, by definition, have more offerings—more departments, more areas of study, more sports, and more extracurricular activities. With size comes real variety.

Yet large schools can also be lonely places. A bigger student body means bigger bureaucracies, making the kind of intimate contact available in a small college (limited to undergraduates) much more difficult. It's not impossible to meet professors, have one-on-one discussions, and take small classes. But it is a lot harder, and the student who succeeds in a big school is generally a go-getter who is not intimidated by size and who seeks out faculty contacts and the many cultural options available on a large campus.

There is also the option of a college within a larger university. Places like Yale, Harvard, and the University of Chicago have undergraduate colleges that offer a smaller and more intimate undergraduate learning environment but benefit from the resources of a much larger university with its graduate and other scholarly and research endeavors.

Religious or Not?

There are roughly 900 four-year religious schools in the country—of every denomination.[8] Many of these schools are conservative and more prescriptive in what they expect of students, faculty, and administrators. A significant number of "A" schools in the American Council of Trustees and Alumni's What Will They Learn? rating are Catholic or evangelical schools, underscoring their commitment to educating in depth across all divisions of knowledge. Schools such as Colorado Christian University and Thomas Aquinas College also have strong codes of conduct for all of their students.[9]

What about Military Service?

Does your child have an interest in enrolling in the Reserve Officers' Training Corps (ROTC) or receiving an ROTC scholarship? The primary purpose of this program, of course, is to produce officers in the military, so anyone who participates in the full ROTC program, or accepts a scholarship, must be prepared for four to ten years of active service after graduation.

Although most Ivy League schools banned ROTC during and after the Vietnam War, many have in recent years invited the programs back to campus.[10] But beware: Ivies can be begrudging when it comes to giving college credit. Harvard ROTC cadets get no credit for ROTC courses, and it's often hard to find courses dedicated to military science or history. Penn students who participate in Naval ROTC do gain credit toward majors in certain academic units.[11] Yale also allows some ROTC classes to count for credit, provided they are shown to be appropriately rigorous.[12]

Gender Distribution

Many don't realize it, but the proportion of women in college has been growing while the proportion of men has been on the decline. There are many reasons for this.[13] But whatever the cause, this means that many schools have a substantial gender imbalance in their undergraduate student populations. Take a look at the websites of colleges you care about, if this matters to you. At the University of North Carolina–Chapel Hill, for example, the ratio of women to men is fifty-eight to forty-two.[14]

Student Success

One measure of a good college is the extent of real learning. As previously noted, many students today are graduating with minimal or no learning gains. How can you tell if schools you're considering are doing a good job? The short answer is it's hard. There are three widely available, affordable, and nationally normed survey tools designed to assess what students know and are able to do. They are known as the Collegiate Learning Assessment (CLA), the Educational Testing Service Proficiency Profile, and the ACT Collegiate Assessment of Academic Proficiency.

For just a few thousand dollars, it's possible for schools to administer these exams to determine whether they are doing a good job and to assess where they can improve. Indeed, the CLA is the instrument of choice for the outcomes assessment project of the thirty-one nations in the Organization of Economic Cooperation and Development.

Knowing how one's doing is, for most people, key to knowing where one's going. But not higher education. For decades, many in the higher education establishment have fought efforts by trustees, administrators, and policymakers to be more open about performance. They've argued that liberal education can't be measured, that students have different and varying skills, and that publishing performance will disadvantage schools with more challenging populations.

While there is some truth to all these objections, students and families rightly want more information, not less. So it's not surprising that, in recent years, there has been a growing concern that the higher education industry has said "trust us" for far too long. During the administration of President George W. Bush, then education secretary Margaret Spellings decided she had had enough. She wanted to know why American students weren't doing better and why costs were so high. Her saber-rattling did get the higher education community excited—and prompted a voluntary effort to provide more information, known as the Voluntary System of Accountability.

Most schools don't collect the information, or if they do, they decline to share it. You can find information on those schools that do participate at http://www.collegeportraits.org/ or at www.whatwilltheylearn.com.

Your best bet may be to look at the pass rates on standardized licensure examinations, which can sometimes be found on the college website under "Student Right to Know." Another option is to examine the percentage of students who are hired shortly after graduation, again sometimes available on college websites.[15] There is also the informative website of PayScale, www.payscale.com, which tracks alumni outcomes in the marketplace. While the goal of education is more than getting a job, in the absence of robust student learning assessments, success in the job market can be a healthy proxy for educational value.

Given the trillions of dollars we are spending on higher education, it's frankly hard to believe that parents and policymakers are pretty much left in the dark when it comes to knowing what students are learning. That's why I urge you to demand greater accountability when it comes to student performance in the postscript of this book.

Admissions Prospects

One thing you will also want to consider is your child's prospects for admission. You can find out by looking at the deadlines for applications and the number of students accepted. At Princeton, for example, in 2016, 29,303 applied by the January 1 deadline and a mere 1,894 (6.46 percent) got in.[16] At Clemson, by contrast, the deadline for the academic year is May 1—quite late—and over half (11,483 out of 22,396) got in in 2015, meaning that a student has a much better chance of being accepted at this public university.[17]

THE ELITES AND HONORS COLLEGES

Professor Andrew Hacker and Claudia Dreifus call them the "Golden Dozen"—Harvard, Yale, Princeton, Stanford, Brown, Dartmouth, Columbia, Cornell, Penn, Duke, Amherst, and Williams. Together, they enrolled just

Figure 2.1.   **Widener Library, Harvard College.** *Source*: Peter Spiro/Getty Images.

under 1 percent of the nationals entering class in 2010.[18] And yet they have an outsized impact on the discussion of American higher education and the college-selection process.

Let's start with the numbers. The fact is that it's hard to get into these schools, no matter how good you are! In 2016, Harvard boasted 39,041 applicants; 5.4 percent were offered places—for a total of 2,106 students.[19] Stanford—even more competitive—received 42,497 applicants and accepted 2,142.[20] These schools receive and recruit applicants from around the country and the globe. And there is simply nothing comparable to the dog-eat-dog world engendered by the Ivy League application process.

The University of Virginia and the University of Texas–Austin are both highly selective public flagships, but their numbers pale by comparison. In 2015–2016, for example, Virginia had 30,840 applicants and admitted 9,186, or 30 percent. In 2015–2016, Texas reported a 45 percent in-state acceptance rate and a 29 percent out-of-state rate.[21]

So what's a family to do? While the "golden dozen" may be right for some, those who turn elsewhere should not despair.

The survey, What Will They Learn?, for the most part, gives these schools low grades when it comes to general education. Of the twelve schools, four receive a D or F for failing to require students to take foundational courses in U.S. history, literature, economics, and math. Only three—Columbia, Cornell, and Duke—receive above-average grades. And only Columbia requires a survey course in literature and a course on US history or government.

It's true that GenEd is only one piece of any college curriculum, and a failure to offer a coherent core is not the end of the equation. But it is noteworthy that, in recent years, students and faculty at Harvard complained—and complained loudly—that the curriculum was lacking in both theme and thoughtfulness.

In days gone by, these elite colleges expected rigorous tests and oral exams before students could graduate. But now Princeton is alone in requiring all of its seniors to complete a thesis. And while some majors still require an oral exam and a thesis for students to graduate with distinction, the days of institution-wide rigorous assessments are over. When last reported, the median grade at Harvard was A-, and the grade given most frequently was A.

High-profile alumni of the elites are the first to credit their professional and personal success to the friendships they made and the contacts they developed at these schools. And, there is no question that these schools are some of the wealthiest in the country, making resources and options available to students simply without parallel.

But more than a few folks in the know have concluded that many institutions may provide more affordable options with a real return than the Ivy League. Journalist Jon Levine even went so far as to say that "while many graduates of these prestigious schools embark on careers of fabulous wealth, not getting admitted is, in many ways, a blessing in disguise."

Why, you ask? Because, particularly for students who receive no or limited financial aid, better value may lie elsewhere. Using the website, PayScale, Levine takes a look at the potential future earnings of students at a range of colleges. Harvard's median annual return on investment (ROI), we learn, is 7.1 percent, putting it a good ways down the list.

Indeed, as Levine relates, plenty of America's universities, both public and private, "require much less from students financially, and deliver a lot more." His favorites include: Georgia Institute of Technology, Rice University, University of Maryland, Harvey Mudd, and Berkeley, to name a few.[22]

There are also appealing—and potentially far more affordable—alternatives available to students through honors colleges at state flagship universities. *New York Times* columnist Frank Bruni tells the tale of one Ronald Nelson, who turned down Harvard, Yale, and Princeton to attend the University of Alabama's honors program.[23] There, for a far smaller price tag, Nelson enjoyed small classes and an intimate experience in the midst of a large and diverse university.

And there's even some evidence that Ivy League schools actually add little value outside social networking. In *Academically Adrift*, the book mentioned in chapter 1, Professors Arum and Roksa note that there is more difference within schools when it comes to student learning gains than between schools, meaning that some students can go to Harvard and Yale and learn very little.

The American Council of Trustees and Alumni (ACTA) conducted a survey of students in the most highly ranked and selective colleges in the country back in 2000 and found that they were amazingly ignorant when it came to basic facts of history and government. And a more recent Intercollegiate Studies Institute survey documented student learning loss—not gain—among Ivy League graduates during their college years.

In recent years, there has also been a robust debate about the mind-set of many Ivy League students, prompted by a *New Republic* article by William Deresiewicz, who taught at Yale for twenty years. According to Deresiewicz, the Ivy League student bodies are like sheep, hence the title of his hard-hitting book, *Excellent Sheep: The Miseducation of the American Elite and the Way to a Meaningful Life*. Deresiewicz has little good to say about the Ivy League, writing that Ivy League schools and their peer institutions do little to engender moral values. Rather, they "manufacture young people who are smart and talented and driven, yes, but also anxious, timid, and lost, with little intellectual curiosity and a student sense of purpose."

Another grad sees a different problem. Stanford alumnus and PayPal inventor Peter Thiel is so concerned that elite institutions waste many bright students' time that he has made an alternative available, what is known as the Thiel Fellowship. On an annual basis, he awards $100,000 to twenty people under twenty years old to leave college behind and pursue their own ventures.

So, the long and short of it: If you aren't paying, there are few downsides—and many upsides—to having a family member attend the Ivy League. With care and attention, one can receive an excellent education, have the opportunity to work closely with a big-name professor, and make contacts for life. If you are paying—and taking out substantial debt to do so—you are well advised to be "open" to a range of options. The fact is that there are numerous institutions that offer students a rigorous academic experience, an enjoyable extracurricular life, and an environment that puts students first.

Remember the college-selection process is not about you. It's about finding the right schools that will best help your child earn a living and live a meaningful life.

DOES ACCREDITATION MATTER?

You've seen it, I'm sure. Ads on TV, banners on the website: This school "is accredited by the Western Association of Schools and Colleges." This school "is accredited by the Southern Association of Colleges and Schools"

Federal financial aid will not flow unless a school is accredited. So this "certification" is a life-or-death determination for most colleges and universities. But you shouldn't rely on it when making a choice about academic value.

For a long time, accreditation was considered a good housekeeping seal of approval. But many schools with very low graduation rates and poor performance are accredited—one reason that Congress is currently looking at major reforms.

If a student goes to Harvard, he or she is likely to graduate in four years; 86 percent do. At Western New Mexico State University, only 4 percent of first-time, full-time students graduate within four years.[24] Yet both are accredited.

So don't just look to see if a school is accredited. There is a lot more information that can help you assess a school's quality: curriculum, grad rates, speech codes, and much more. The next few chapters will outline important considerations that should undergird your college-selection process.

OTHER CONSIDERATIONS

COMMUNITY COLLEGES

We live in a culture that assumes a four-year college is good for everyone. But there is no reason that every student needs to start at a four-year residential college. Do community colleges represent an option worth exploring?

The short answer is yes.

As a general rule, community colleges offer an affordable and desirable option, especially so if you are in a state like Tennessee, Massachusetts, Florida, California, or Virginia. In these states, students are guaranteed admission into a four-year in-state school upon completion of a community college associate's degree and upon meeting certain basic standards.[25] Even if you are interested in the Ivy League, community college may still be an option. It used to be that transfer into these schools was virtually impossible, but no more. Princeton, for example, has recently modified its admissions practices to admit transfer students more liberally.[26]

For those who want to pursue a four-year degree, community college can give you two affordable years to explore academic likes and dislikes before transferring to a four-year school. It's an option well worth investigating.

FOR-PROFIT SCHOOLS

For-profit colleges—sometimes called proprietary schools—are another option. These are commercial operations.

For-profit schools charge tuition bills and often earn a large part of their revenue in the form of federal financial aid payments made to students who enroll. Under what is known as the 90/10 rule, for-profits may receive up to 90 percent of their funds from federal aid and be allowed to operate. The University of Phoenix, for example, earned 84 percent of its revenue through financial aid programs in 2012.[27]

Typically, for-profit schools offer certificate and vocational programs (massage, plumbing, etc.) as well as undergraduate and graduate degrees. Some have developed programs particularly suited to nontraditional students who work or go to school part-time.

The quality and stability of for-profit schools can vary widely, much like nonprofit schools. Many are good, many not so. Some are accredited, others not. Some are honest, others take advantage of students through dishonest recruitment strategies and other means.[28]

For some students, for-profits offer a very good option and should not be left out of the equation when looking at the higher education terrain.[29]

VOCATIONAL EDUCATION

If your child likes to work with his or her hands and finds coursework more tedious than challenging, you may want to take a close look at vocational education as an appealing option. States have licensing programs in fields like automobile repair, plumbing, HVAC, and dental hygiene that don't require a college degree and can often be satisfied by less than two years of study.

Educator and author Mark Phillips emphasizes the nation's strong need for vocational education: "Many of the skills most needed to compete in the global market of the 21st century are technical skills that fall into the technical/vocational area. The absence of excellence in many technical and vocational fields is also costing us economically as a nation."

Not everyone needs to go to a four-year school, and those who don't should not be treated with disdain or disapproval by parents and teachers. As Phillips points out, we should make it our business to develop "basic verbal and mathematical literacy for all students" *and* to encourage and cultivate "bodily-kinesthetic and spatial intelligence" among students who gravitate to the trades.[30]

COMPETENCY-BASED PROGRAMS

Also consider alternative programs like Western Governors University (WGU). WGU is not a residential college; it is structured on a promising alternative credentialing system called competency-based education where credit is given for proof of knowledge and skills, not for credit hours or time spent in the classroom.[31] In a competency-based program, students can progress as quickly as they can learn online. And because competency-based programs give credit for prior learning as demonstrated on entrance exams, a student who is very strong in some subjects may be able to test out of many degree requirements.

SUMMING UP

Bottom line: Today's world of higher education is quite different from what it was even twenty years ago. Online offerings and other innovative—and often unbundled—course-based providers are growing more and more prevalent, and with that, there are more choices for families. In this fast-moving world, you'll be better able to make the right match if you and your child are honest with yourselves and resolute about determining why your child is pursuing postsecondary education—and what makes sense.

DOING RESEARCH

Chapter 3

Insist on Academic Substance

What do students learn? You won't find this question in the *U.S. News & World Report* college rankings.[1] But let me suggest that *this* is the most important question of all when it comes to picking a college. Yes, there are many reasons students go to college—and there are many reasons to pick a particular school. But the first consideration should be: Is this school doing a good job of preparing students for informed citizenship, effectiveness in the workforce, and lifelong learning?

Think about this. When asked about their college experience, recent college graduates responded—in large numbers—that they wished they had had a more coherent education. When polled, 80 percent of those surveyed, ages twenty-five to thirty-four, including a significant proportion of recent college graduates, responded that all students should "take basic classes in core subjects."[2] They seemed to recognize, in the face of stark economic reality, that a strong and coherent curriculum would have provided them with the skills and knowledge they need to compete in the job market.

About a third of recent college graduates said they were not prepared for the world of work; more than half said they would pick a different major—or school—or both, if they were to start over. And half of the graduates admitted they did not look at graduation rates when picking a college, while four in ten said they ignored job placement and salary records.[3]

Of course, demanding academic substance is just plain common sense. Of course, a student should have a coherent curriculum. Of course, a college should prepare students for success after graduation.

What's going on?

Until the 1960s, most institutions insisted on rigorous, structured curricula that ensured students a broad, general education, beyond simply their major concentration.[4] These courses—often called a core—exposed students to the array of key events, ideas, and great works—material considered central to a strong education.

Students had some say in their experience, such as in their choice of which foreign language to study, but, generally, the content of their studies was dictated by the school, with the goal of ensuring all students would have classes in the subjects that defined a well-educated person.[5] Faculty and administrators gave priority to what is great and what is essential for students to know and be able to do.

Today, at first glance, schools still maintain the façade of a general education curriculum, through so-called distribution requirements, in which students are required to take courses in several subject groupings outside of their major.[6]

But distribution requirements do not a core curriculum make. Under the distribution requirements scheme, students are typically asked only to take one to three courses in each of five or six broad areas: physical and natural sciences, humanities, social sciences, writing composition, mathematics, and multicultural studies. They may have dozens or even hundreds of courses, oftentimes quite narrow, to choose from within each distribution area. In fact, many colleges brazenly boast about the choices they offer.[7] Here are just a few of the gems that students can take to satisfy distribution requirements.

Horror films and American culture
University of Colorado
"U.S. Context" requirement

Mental illness in the media
The golden age of TV
Elmira College
"U.S. culture and civilization" requirement

Game of Thrones
University of Illinois–Springfield
"Humanities" requirement

Vampires and Other Horrors in Film and Media
University of California–Davis
"American culture, governance, and history" requirement

The Economics of Star Trek
Linfield College
"U.S. pluralisms or individuals, systems, and society" requirement

Food Talks: The Language of Food
Stanford University
"Thinking matters" requirement

Figure 3.1. Goofy Courses That Meet General Education Requirements. *Source:* American Council of Trustees and Alumni.

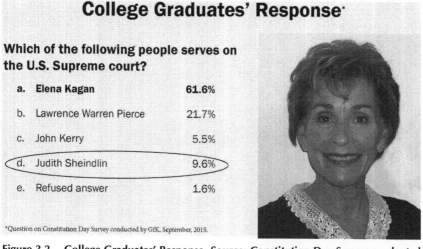

College Graduates' Response*

Which of the following people serves on the U.S. Supreme court?

a.	Elena Kagan	**61.6%**
b.	Lawrence Warren Pierce	21.7%
c.	John Kerry	5.5%
d.	Judith Sheindlin	9.6%
e.	Refused answer	1.6%

*Question on Constitution Day Survey conducted by GfK, September, 2015.

Figure 3.2. College Graduates' Response. *Source:* Constitution Day Survey conducted by GfK for the American Council of Trustees and Alumni, September 8, 2015.

Most schools today, frankly, leave it up to students to devise their own curricula. Do-it-yourself for $250,000! Indeed, there are many in the academy who think content is not really important; instead, it is "critical thinking" that matters.

In my experience, though, it's hard to think critically if you have nothing to think critically about. And, not surprisingly, surveys confirm that the "anything goes" curricular model that rules on most campuses is failing to provide students with the knowledge and skills they need.

The National Assessment of Adult Literacy, a test administered by the U.S. Department of Education, found that the majority of college graduates were below proficient in basic literary and math skills, meaning they could not correctly compare the perspectives in two editorials or compute the cost of food items. A Lumina Foundation/Gallup study documented substantial employer unhappiness; indeed, two-thirds of business leaders surveyed did not believe that recent college graduates had the skillsets they needed for their businesses.[8]

The cafeteria-style approach that now reigns on most college campuses is a poor substitute for a true, carefully designed general education curriculum. Because an eighteen-year-old's judgment is apt to be untutored, and because most college guidance systems are ineffective, students can graduate with vast gaps in their skills and knowledge. It is not surprising, then, that employers are complaining!

Fortunately, there is a wonderful website that will show you which schools have a coherent general education curriculum and which don't. The American Council of Trustees and Alumni's (ACTA) website www.whatwilltheylearn.

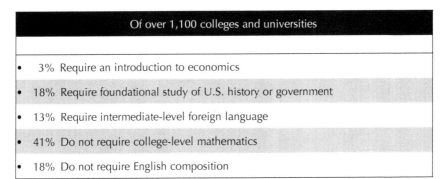

Of over 1,100 colleges and universities
• 3% Require an introduction to economics
• 18% Require foundational study of U.S. history or government
• 13% Require intermediate-level foreign language
• 41% Do not require college-level mathematics
• 18% Do not require English composition

Figure 3.3. What Will They Learn?—ACTA's 2016–2017 Study of the Core Curriculum. *Source:* **American Council of Trustees and Alumni.**

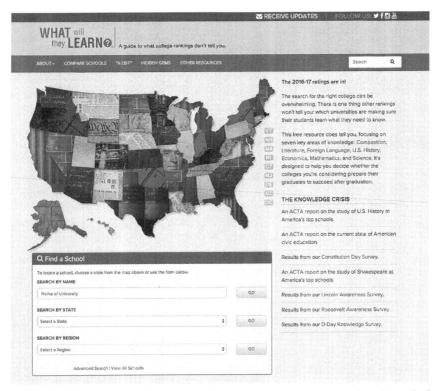

Figure 3.4. *What Will They Learn?* **Website's Home Page.** *Source:* **American Council of Trustees and Alumni.**

com looks at virtually every college or university in the country that purports to have a liberal arts mission.

What Will They Learn? grades schools according to a modest set of expectations. It assesses schools on whether students will be exposed to seven core subjects before they graduate: expository writing, a survey of literature, intermediate-level foreign language, U.S. history or government, economics, mathematics, and natural science.[9]

The seven core courses can be provided in thirty credits or fewer and offer students a strong foundation while still affording them ample choice. There is little reason for a school not to meet these modest expectations. But most don't.

As you start the selection process, look and see which schools offer strong foundations. *What Will They Learn?* profiles twenty-five "A" schools around the country, schools that require students to take at least six of the seven core subjects outlined. And there are more than 350 schools that earn a "B"; these schools expect students to take at least four of the seven core subjects outlined.[10] A strong general education curriculum is evidence that the adults on campus have thoughtfully asked and answered the question of what graduates should be expected to know and be able to do. That's no doubt why Christopher Newport University decided to take out full-color ads in the *Washington Post* and *Richmond Times-Dispatch* highlighting its core curriculum.

Instead of talking about shows on cable or TV, students at schools that have strong core curricula can have a common *intellectual* conversation—a

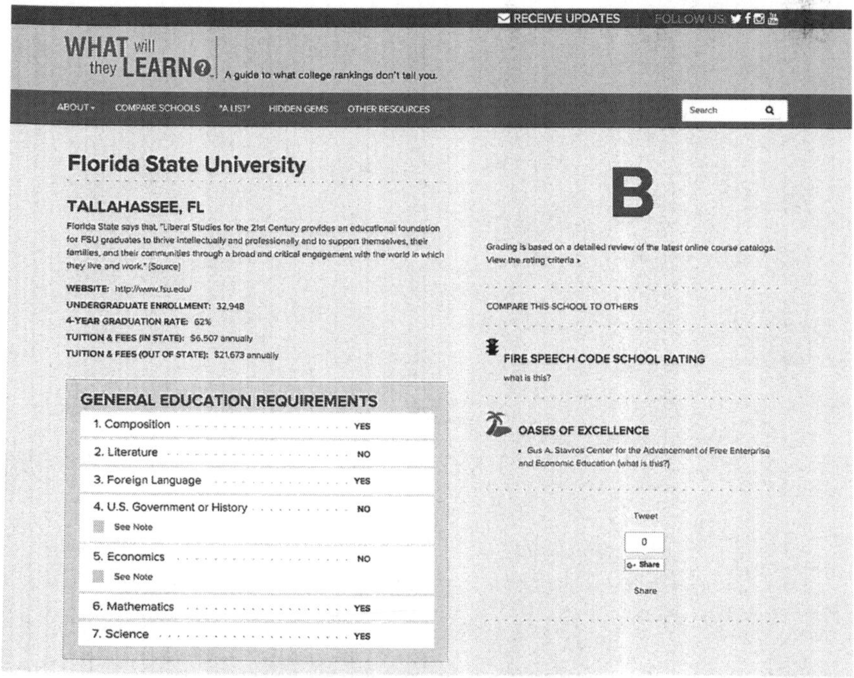

Figure 3.5. What Will They Learn? Website's Grading of Florida States University. *Source:* American Council of Trustees and Alumni.

Schools Receiving an "A" Grade for a Core Curriculum

www.whatwilltheylearn.com

- Baylor University
- Bluefield College
- California Polytechnic State University–San Luis Obispo
- Christopher Newport University
- Clark Atlanta University
- Colorado Christian University
- Gardner–Webb University
- Georgia Southern University
- Kennesaw State University
- Morehouse College
- Pepperdine University
- Regent University
- Saint Katherine College
- Southwest Baptist University
- St. John's College (MD)
- St. John's College (NM)
- Thomas Aquinas College
- Thomas More College of Liberal Arts
- United States Air Force Academy
- United States Coast Guard Academy
- United States Merchant Marine Academy
- United States Military Academy
- University of Dallas
- University of Georgia
- University of Science and Arts of Oklahoma

Figure 3.6.   Schools Receiving an "A" Grade for Core Curricula. *Source:* www.whatwill theylearn.com.

discussion about the great books they are all reading, not who was chosen on *The Bachelor*. A strong core also ensures broad skills and knowledge that will help students maneuver within the rapidly changing marketplace.

Even if the schools you explore do not have strong general education curricula, your child can still build a good foundation by selecting courses that will prepare him or her for success after graduation. You should encourage him or her to design a general education program that provides exposure to key subjects—math, science, literature, composition, history, and foreign language—even if they are not required.

WHAT ABOUT MAJORS?

It is good to examine colleges and universities' major offerings as well. Go to their websites and look for academics, courses of instruction, undergraduate programs, academic bulletin, or similarly named resources.

Find the fields with which you are most familiar. Take history, for example. Does the school expect history majors to study a breadth of historical fields—world, American, and Eastern history? Or can the student simply pick and choose, making up the major as he or she goes along or satisfying requirements with narrow topics? At Amherst, for example, a student majoring in history needs to complete nine courses in his or her major, but coursework in U.S. or European history is optional.[11] At the University of Wisconsin–Madison, students can earn a history degree without ever taking a course in American history.[12]

Look at the breadth of subfields as well. Can you find courses on military history or diplomatic history? Or are most of the courses dealing with topics such as race, class, or gender?

Acclaimed Brooklyn College Professor of History Robert "KC" Johnson has analyzed the academic structure of history departments at top public institutions around the country, and his findings are well worth thinking about.

Over the last generation, he writes, "the percentage of professors trained in areas of US history some would deem 'traditional' and others would dismiss as the study of 'dead white men' has plummeted. . . . [E]ven those who remain in the subfields often have 're-visioned' their topics to make them little more than a permutation on the race/class/gender approach that dominates the contemporary historical profession. The result is that even those students who want to encounter courses taught by those trained in US political, diplomatic, constitutional, or military history are unable to do so."[13] So check this out.

Do the same when it comes to other subjects. Let's say your child is thinking about majoring in English. Then he or she should expect Shakespeare,

Milton, Melville, Twain, and more. Right? Maybe, or maybe not. A 2015 report, *The Unkindest Cut: Shakespeare in Exile 2015*, finds that students in the most elite—and expensive—colleges can graduate without ever taking a course devoted to Shakespeare, let alone studying Milton or Chaucer.[14]

By looking at what is required, you can generally get a good idea about what professors in the department value and whether your child will be encouraged to explore the classics of great literature or be pointed to victim studies and books heavy on postmodernist theory and ideology rather than what William Faulkner called the "old verities and truths of the heart."[15]

Information about general education and major requirements can truly help complete the "value" question and offer crucial insights into institutions' ability to ensure your child's success. Ask good questions, and pointed ones if necessary, when it comes to academic quality. The following checklist includes a number of vital issues regarding academic excellence to explore.

FIND OUT

- Does a school's curriculum ensure an orderly progression from elementary to advanced levels of knowledge?
- Do general education requirements guarantee a basic knowledge of math and the physical and biological sciences; foreign language; literature; economics; composition; and the foundations and principles of American society?
- How does the institution program the freshman year for student success?
- Do advisors have regular contact with students to help with curricular planning and course selection? How often?
- Are the advisors faculty members, or is advising delegated to support staff?
- Does the school have an online planning tool that will help students map out all four years and avoid delays in graduation?
- Do students write substantial essays at every stage and must they demonstrate their proficiency in formal written English?
- Does the school monitor student progress? Does it have an early warning system to spot and address academic weaknesses? How is this done?
- Do tenured faculty members, including senior ones (who have titles such as professor or associate professor), teach introductory courses as well as advanced seminars for majors, and are they regularly engaged in academic counseling?
- Does the school have a clear, published policy defining its commitment to liberty of thought and freedom of speech?
- Does the school make available assessment results documenting student learning and achievements?
- What does the school do to ensure that "gateway" courses (those courses that are required for entry into major programs) are a successful experience

for students with uneven levels of preparation? Are there special programs for students who enter with limited proficiency in mathematics?
- Are there enough sections of required and gateway courses so that students are not kept from graduating in four years due to course bottlenecks?
- Are there opportunities to engage with faculty—such as a sustained research project?

FOR THE LOVE OF STEM

Make no mistake about it: American business leaders and policymakers at every level love STEM. STEM is the rather gawky acronym for science, technology, engineering, and math. More and more studies outline how the United States is falling behind when it comes to the sophisticated skills these majors supply and that the economy needs.

Employers are looking for graduates in these fields; Congress is looking for national expertise. And it's generally, but not always, the case that students who graduate in these fields—or have made their way through a strong general education curriculum that includes STEM fields—will do well when it comes to getting a job.[16]

According to Jim Tankersley, a *Washington Post* reporter of economic policy, Department of Labor data show that "[t]he average starting salary for an engineering major [in 2012] was $62,655, tops among the eight categories of majors tracked in the study. In 2009, at the end of the Great Recession, the unemployment rate for math and computer science grads a year removed from earning their degrees was six percent—half the rate for humanities or social science majors."[17]

Interestingly, large numbers of students start out their college careers intending to major in a STEM field. At Harvard, for instance, 51 percent of freshmen respondents entering in fall 2015 said they would pursue a major in the sciences, engineering, or applied sciences.[18] But many never get to the finish line. Research by economists at Berea College and the University of Western Ontario suggests that "fewer than half of the students who start out as science majors end up earning a science degree."[19]

There are surely many reasons, but one is that students often find that majoring in these fields is tough. There is no question that "As" abound in the humanities and social sciences, while the STEM fields remain much more rigorous. Students understandably game the system to avoid more difficult subjects and to keep their postgraduation options open. It is also true that many times students arrive unprepared for the gateway courses that are key to advancement in the field.[20]

Some schools are much better than others at ensuring student success in their chosen fields. At the University of Notre Dame, for example, the faculty redesigned gateway chemistry and engineering courses when they discovered that too many students were dropping out and abandoning their plans for the future. Rather than creating a "sink or swim" environment, they aimed to create a culture committed to excellent teaching and student success.[21] Asking about gateway courses and student performance is a good way to explore an institution's academic quality.

You know, better than the college, whether your son or daughter has a knack for science and math. If he or she does, encourage persistence and hard work; insist that grades are important but that undertaking a challenging course of study is even more important to future success.

The Science Crisis

"We should take no pride in a finding that 70 percent of Americans cannot read and understand the science section of the *New York Times*."

Jon Miller, Michigan State University
John A. Hannah Professor of Integrative Studies
American Association for the Advancement of Science Symposium, February 27, 2007

Figure 3.7. The Science Crisis. *Source:* Jon Miller, Michigan State University, John A. Hannah Professor of Integrative Studies, American Association for the Advancement of Science Symposium, February 27, 2007.

SUMMING UP

As you prepare to select a college, one thing should be clear: the most important reason to pick a school is academic excellence. Too many students—after they have graduated—wish they had pursued a more coherent curriculum ensuring a strong foundation of skills and knowledge. Armed with the questions in this chapter, you and your child can zero in on real academic substance and seriousness. You'll be glad you did.

Chapter 4

Look for Serious and Responsible Teaching

So, we've looked at the general education curriculum and majors. Next, you're going to want to look for serious teaching.

Here's a quick primer.

IDENTIFY THE FACULTY

For starters, find the professors. Go to the departmental pages of the college's website, where you can typically find their names, degrees held (and sometimes the schools from which the professors graduated), titles, and academic specialties. Adjunct faculty are the lowest on the totem pole; they have only short-term contracts and no hope of tenure. Assistant professors come next, looking for tenure, but with no job protection. Associate and full professors are almost always tenured—that means they have taught and pursued research for at least seven years and have been granted lifelong job protection.

Famed historian of ancient Greece Donald Kagan established an important teaching doctrine: When he was dean of Yale College, he made it known that he wanted senior faculty to teach the introductory courses, with the understanding that it takes a mature, comprehensive view of the field to do these courses well. As he saw it, survey courses should not be left to the most inexperienced faculty, whose training has typically been specialized.[1] And Professor Kagan walked the walk: His introductory course on the history of ancient Greece was legendary—not to mention demanding and comprehensive.[2]

A scientist who took the same path is Carl Wieman, the holder of a joint appointment in physics and education at Stanford. This outstanding professor won a Nobel Prize in physics and could have pursued a career entirely devoted to research science. Instead, he devotes himself to undergraduate science education and has pioneered the use of experimental techniques to evaluate what teaching methods work best.[3]

Identifying just who is teaching can tell you a lot about whether your child will hear from the school's academic stars or is more likely to spend time interacting with adjunct faculty, teaching assistants (TAs), and graduate students seeking their PhDs. Of course, adjuncts and TAs can often be excellent teachers. So that need not be determinative, but think hard about an institution that delegates most teaching to faculty who only hold short-term contracts.

And here's another caveat that applies to all levels of college teachers: The sad fact is that many schools prioritize faculty research over good teaching, putting students at a real disadvantage when it comes to engagement in the classroom. One scholar has documented how research "productivity" has skyrocketed over time, with the number of academic publications increasing 500 percent from 1959 to 2009.

Figure 4.1. Indiana University–Bloomington Department of English Sample Faculty Profile.

At the same time, it's not surprising that undergraduate performance has been declining. As one education expert has noted, "The established hiring and tenure systems encourage young professors and graduate students to zero in on research and devote little attention to the collegiate classroom."[4] So try to get a clear sense of whether the school seeks and rewards good teaching.

Also take a look at faculty profiles, which you can often reach under the "Academics" sections of college websites. Look at faculty in a range of fields—history, economics, women's studies, biology, and so on.

Do the professors' backgrounds reflect quality and range? Are their academic interests and specialties likely to ensure students obtain the foundational knowledge they need, or are they more focused on the professor's hobbyhorses—and political views—rather than student needs?

What do students think of them? While it's not definitive, you can find student assessments of many professors—including whether they explain their subjects in an effective way—at www.ratemyprofessors.com. At some schools, you will be able to find a lot. At others, very little.

Remember: this investigation of faculty and courses is the same exercise your child will want to undertake when he or she is actually putting together a course schedule. So sit down and practice this together!

THEN LOOK AT COURSE LISTINGS

For each class, course listings (Figure 4.2) should give you the name of the teacher, the frequency of class meetings, the credits offered, and sometimes the size of the class. Then you'll want to find the syllabus—the listing of class requirements and readings—which is often posted online. It is old news that the actual topics and readings for a course do not always match the catalog description. And syllabi can tell you a lot about the breadth and balance of courses offered.

The unpleasant truth is that there is often a troubling lack of balance and intellectual openness when it comes to class reading requirements. Pick up almost any newspaper—or listen to accounts on cable news—and you'll likely hear stories about the political imbalance on campuses: courses offering only one perspective, conservatives feeling under siege, surveys documenting a veritable monolith when it comes to faculty viewpoints, and political affiliation.

Perhaps that's why 42 percent of students surveyed some years ago at the *U.S. News & World Report*'s top twenty-five liberal arts colleges and top twenty-five universities complained that some course readings showed only one side of a controversial issue. And almost one-third (29 percent) believed they had to agree with the professor to get a good grade.[5]

University Catalog 2016-2017

UNIVERSITY OF COLORADO BOULDER

General Information   Programs of Study   Colleges & Schools   Admission   **Courses**

Home / Courses

Courses

Search by College, Department & Category

College/School
Arts & Sciences

Department
Art and Art History

Category
Art History

Search

Search by Course Number

Subject   Number

Search

ARTH-1300 (3) History of World Art 1

Surveys major art styles from the Paleolithic period through the Renaissance, including European, Asian, and the Pre-Columbian/Islamic world. Emphasizes comparison of Western and non-Western visual expressions as evidence of differing cultural orientations. Approved for GT-AH1. Approved for arts and sciences core curriculum: literature and the arts.

Arts & Sciences   Art and Art History   Art History

ARTH-1400 (3) History of World Art 2

Surveys major art styles from about 1600 to the present, including Europe, Asia, the Islamic world, the Americas, and tribal arts. Emphasizes comparison of Western and non-Western visual expressions as evidence of differing cultural orientations. Credit not granted for this course and FINE 1409. Approved for GT-AH1. Approved for arts and sciences core curriculum: literature and the arts.

Figure 4.2.   CU University Catalog 2016–2017. Sample Course Listing.

Nearly 60 percent (57.5 percent) of students, when given virtually the same questions at Idaho colleges and universities, found that various courses on their campus "had readings that present only one side of a controversial issue." In Missouri, it was much the same: 56.8 percent; in Georgia, 55.3 percent; in Illinois, 61 percent; in Maine, 60.9 percent.[6] In each case, more than half! The one-sidedness of reading assignments has evidently contributed to a chill in the classroom climate: In 2015, a national undergraduate study conducted by McLaughlin & Associates found that 49 percent of students surveyed felt intimidated when offering beliefs that differed from their professors.[7]

So what's a parent to do? For starters, here are questions you will want to ask to help determine whether the school is fostering responsible and balanced teaching:

- Is the course description clear—or is it jargon-ridden or tendentious?
- Is the reading list substantive and balanced or do the readings present only

one side of a controversial issue? Are social or political issues presented fairly, with attention to divergent perspectives in the field?
• Does the reading list include primary source documents—for example, do the students read the *Federalist Papers* themselves or just textbook summaries of them?

Sometimes, syllabi can be found easily on public pages. Sometimes syllabi are included in the professor's online profile. In many cases, access to syllabi is possible only through a login password.

If you happen to be looking at Texas public schools, you are in luck. Because it is often so hard to find out what professors are teaching, the Texas legislature in 2009 adopted a syllabi bill designed to let taxpayers and students see exactly what they are paying for.[8] In the Lone Star State, all you have to do is go to a college website and search for syllabi! Voila! They are at your fingertips.

And, for those outside of Texas, there is a new and growing resource called the Open Syllabus Explorer. It doesn't provide the syllabus itself, but it does allow you to see what books are most frequently assigned at schools—public and private—around the country.[9]

OASES OF EXCELLENCE

You should also look for what one organization has dubbed *oases of excellence*.[10] (see Figure 4.3). These are special programs on campuses that often offer superior alternatives to the regular campus fare. In far too many places, the trendy has supplanted the important. Courses on pop culture, sex, and current politics abound—such as "The Graphic Novel" and "Seminar in Criticism and Theory: Animals, Cannibals, Vegetables"—while courses on Plato or Adam Smith may be far and few between.[11]

Ideally, colleges and universities expose students to a wide range of viewpoints and perspectives. But too often, campuses fall short. The "oases" offer students excellent programs, courses, debates, and lectures with high intellectual standards that have not been politicized or dumbed down. They offer an opportunity to draw young people into the life of the mind on topics such as Great Books, capitalism, and Western civilization.

COMMUNITY SERVICE REQUIREMENTS

Increasingly, students are required to fulfill a "community service" requirement. While it sounds good—who doesn't believe in community service?—in fact this community service often comes with a political agenda.

BROWN UNIVERSITY
Political Theory Project
By using both humanistic and social scientific tools, Brown University's Political Theory Project seeks to "invigorate the study of institutions and ideas that make societies free." It regularly sponsors speakers and offers postdoctoral fellowships as well as undergraduate courses. The student arm of the project is the Janus Forum, which sponsors a public lecture series, luncheon discussions, and public debates. The Political Theory Project was founded in 2003, and is currently directed by John Tomasi.

CLEMSON UNIVERSITY
Clemson Institute for the Study of Capitalism
The mission of the Clemson Institute for the Study of Capitalism is to "increase public awareness of the moral foundations of capitalism." It sponsors an undergraduate junior fellows program and a visiting scholars program as well as speakers and conferences throughout the year. The institute was founded in 2005 by the current executive director C. Bradley Thompson.

COLUMBIA UNIVERSITY
Center on Law and Liberty
Columbia Law School announced the creation of the Center on Law and Liberty at the end of 2014. The center was founded to "study freedom, threats to its existence, and legal protections designed to ensure its survival." It is overseen by Philip Hamburger, the Maurice and Hilda Friedman Professor of Law at Columbia Law School and an expert on constitutional law and religious liberty. The Center on Law and Liberty primarily hosts events focused on academic freedom.

FURMAN UNIVERSITY
The Tocqueville Program
Named for the great student of democracy, Alexis de Tocqueville, the Tocqueville Program sponsors courses and brings prominent scholars and public intellectuals to Furman's campus "with the aim of encouraging serious and open engagement with the moral questions at the heart of political life." The program was founded in 2006 thanks to the generosity and tireless efforts of Ginny and Sandy MacNeil. The Tocqueville Program is currently directed by Professors Benjamin Storey and Aristide Tessitore.

ST. OLAF UNIVERSITY
The Institute for Freedom & Community
St. Olaf University's Institute for Freedom & Community began in 2015. Professor Daniel Hofrenning directs the program, which examines important public issues through vigorous, yet civil discourse. Through debate, discussion, and openness to competing viewpoints, students engage the major controversies of our times. The Institute supports St. Olaf University's Public Affairs Conversation: a two-course interdisciplinary study sequence for juniors and seniors: Freedom and Community in the American Experience and Freedom and Community in Ongoing Social and Political Debates. The coursework is supplemented by an internship in business, government, or public service. Outside speakers also energize dialogue on campus throughout the school year.

TEXAS TECH UNIVERSITY
The Institute for the Study of Western Civilization
Texas Tech's Institute for the Study of Western Civilization, which is affiliated with the school's Honors College, sponsors research, teaching, and extracurricular speakers to address "Western Civilization as a distinct phenomenon." It helped develop a concentration in Western Civilization within the Honors Arts and Letters degree program in which students study U.S. and Western history, fine arts, philosophy, logic, science, and the Great Books of the Western world. It is directed by Professor Steve Balch, a founding member of American Council of Trustees and Alumni's board and founding president of the National Association of Scholars.

Figure 4.3. A Sampling of Oases of Excellence. *Source:* www.goacta.org/initiatives/ alumni_to_the_rescue_funding_oases_of_excellence.

Take Bill Felkner, formerly a student in the School of Social Work at Rhode Island College. Felkner chose to work for a Republican governor to fulfill his community service fieldwork requirement. Far from being praised for his engagement, he was denied a degree: faculty claimed that political advocacy for "progressive social change" was a prerequisite of the fieldwork.[12]

Emily Brooker was studying social work at Missouri State University, where a professor required her to sign a letter advocating for homosexual foster parent adoption, to be sent to the state legislature. When she refused to do so, the assignment was made optional. But, shortly thereafter, she found herself charged by the school with a "Level 3" violation—the most serious possible—for failing to uphold professional social work standards. Brooker sued and the school settled for an undisclosed sum.[13]

Too often, it seems, only politically correct projects get approved for community service credits, and typically these are only those involved with government agencies or nonprofits with a more liberal social welfare agenda. One would think that assisting an entrepreneur or even starting a business would be a real community service. But at too many places, these are deemed to be tainted by the profit motive.

SUMMING UP

The best kind of education is one that "liberates" the mind, opening up differing perspectives to students and allowing a free and open exchange of ideas. That's why it is important for families to examine course descriptions, look at faculty profiles, and learn as much as possible about the reading lists and requirements before picking a school. As outlined in this chapter, a growing number of schools are also welcoming vibrant campus centers that offer an alternative to regular campus fare. Identifying schools that embrace serious and responsible teaching should be the foundation of any thoughtful college decision.

Chapter 5

Understand Dorm Life

There is no question that people go to college to become educated. But they also go to college to become adults. From the beginning, the residential college experience has been understood to be a unique "coming-of-age" time for students, an experience that helps to shape character and values. Living in the dorm has been a central part of that experience, allowing students to meet others from varied backgrounds and, ideally, to learn to balance individual freedoms with respect for the rights of others.

We can all agree that residential life offers a unique educational experience. So how can you help your child have the best residential experience?

First, get up to speed. Dorm life today is probably not what you remember.

Since the 1960s, colleges and universities have ceased to function as they had been functioning for centuries—in loco parentis. For decades, college administrators enforced strict expectations for student conduct, thus effectively maintaining a parental role. During the 1960s, however, new legal rulings compelled them to relax the enforcement of rules, such as those previously governing curfews, dormitory guests, and dating.[1] As a consequence, today it's pretty much "anything goes."

For many students, the open-ended campus experience can be transformative. But for others, it can be quite destructive.

Go to the "Residential Life" pages of the colleges you are examining and take a look at what they offer. Be prepared to ask questions. Are students of both sexes expected to share the same room or just the same floor? Are bathrooms single-sex, or are they coed too?

As it turns out, single-sex dormitories are rare. Notre Dame, Brigham Young, and the Catholic University of America (CUA) are three institutions where this arrangement can still be found.[2] In 2011, CUA President John Garvey announced, in a much noted *Wall Street Journal* column, the university's return to single-sex housing, confessing that college administrators had concluded that coed housing was contributing to "a hotbed of reckless drinking and hooking up."[3]

Most schools today have coed housing, and some even have "gender-neutral" housing. Coed housing means men and women live in the same dorm together—sometimes on the same floor or hallway, sometimes in the same suite or room. Villanova and St. Joseph's University have coed residence halls, for example, but not coed dorm rooms.[4]

"Gender-neutral" housing means undergraduates of opposite sexes may share a room.

At least one public university system stands out for its refusal to allow students of both sexes to live together. In the fall of 2013, the board of governors of the University of North Carolina system voted unanimously to ban campuses from letting students of opposite genders live in the same dorm suites or apartments. In North Carolina, under the ban, institutions may still have coed dorms, but students of opposite sexes are not allowed to share suites with common living areas and bathrooms. Advocates for gay and transgendered students protested the decision, while others praised the board for bringing sanity to the campus housing environment.[5]

RESIDENTIAL COMMUNITIES

Many schools also focus residential life on student interests and "communities." Some institutions have substance-free housing (certainly a confession against interest!). Many others have learning communities with special academic foci, such as engineering, a foreign language, or science.

Like many higher education projects, the value of these communities can vary, depending on their execution and guiding principles. Evidence suggests that freshman retention rates and academic achievement levels are often higher among learning-community participants than among nonparticipants. Indeed, the success of the learning-community model inspired CUA's First-Year Experience program, "where learning communities take as their focal point the Western civilization-oriented humanities core curriculum required of all freshmen."[6]

But there can also be serious drawbacks when ideology or lifestyle is the organizing principle. Scholars have concluded that absent sufficient guidance, youthful academic inexperience can devolve into groupthink and intellectual shallowness. The devil is in the details.[7]

Look at the University of Wisconsin–Madison, for example. At this immense flagship university, students are offered the opportunity to apply for learning communities centered on biology, language, and entrepreneurship.[8] There are also a wide range of less traditional communities such as:

- **Green House**—"setting students on paths to find sustainable solutions to social and environmental challenges, exploring food and agrifood systems, conservation and biodiversity, environmental justice, and green business, building and design."[9]
- **The Multicultural Learning Community**—"serving students who have a thirst to understand the problems, issues, benefits, and contributions to human diversity and social justice."[10]
- **Open House: Gender Learning Community**—welcoming all "students who wish to examine both conventional and transformational assumptions about gender and sexuality. Students from all genders, sexualities, and racial/ethnic/cultural backgrounds/disciplines are invited."[11]

WHO DOES THE ADVISING?

At the same time, take a look at who's in charge. Is there evidence that faculty reside and oversee house life to have more interaction with students? Or are personnel largely other students, being paid for the "honor," with little expertise in advising and mentoring? Are they called *student advisors* or do they have other names, such as *community diversity assistants* or *customs people*?[12]

The sad fact is that the growth in administrators and other noninstruction staff today far outpaces the growth in faculty on college campuses.[13] Recent years have seen a proliferation of student life advisors and student affairs staff in particular.[14]

HONOR CODES AND CODES OF CONDUCT

You'll also want to see if the school has an honor code or student code of conduct. These codes offer a perspective on the community's values and concerns. At Smith, for example, the Student Conduct and Responsibility Code says, "Smith is a community founded on individual integrity and respect for others. . . . [L]iving successfully in this community will always depend on balancing the greatest possible freedom for the individual with a sensitivity to and respect for the rights of others."[15] At Hampden-Sydney, the focus is on conducting oneself with integrity and treating one another with civility.[16]

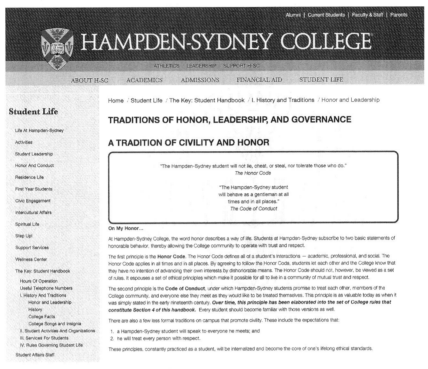

Figure 5.1. Hampden-Sydney College.

DINING HALLS AND FOOD COURTS

Increasingly, college dining halls are yielding to food courts. Burgers, salads, and ethnic foods—a whole range of culinary options—are now available, including foods for those with allergies or vegan predilections.

Some schools have gone "no trays" to help ward against the consumption (or waste) of too much food.[17] Others simply leave it up to students to pick and choose from a range of facilities and foods—without regard to good nutrition or balanced eating habits. To make matters worse, college meal plans that structure student dining are often indifferent, if not downright hostile, to healthy eating habits.[18] That may be why a growing number of families are sending college "care packages" filled with apples and fruits!

SUSTAINABILITY

We can't leave food courts and dining halls without addressing the latest phenomenon: sustainability. It sounds innocent enough, conjuring images of recycling, organic options, and sustainable agricultural practices. But no. The

National Association of Scholars has studied "sustainability" and has concluded that, in its latest incarnation, it entails more than environmental awareness. Their report, *Sustainability: Higher Education's New Fundamentalism*, concludes, in fact, that the promotion of sustainability can severely limit free speech and the robust exchange of ideas.[19]

As they describe it, sustainability "marks out a new and larger ideological territory in which curtailing economic, political, and intellectual liberty is the price that must be paid now to ensure the welfare of future generations." They find that, in many schools, adherence to "sustainability" has resulted in limiting the freedom of students to inquire, marginalizing and branding students who dare raise a question as "climate deniers."

And they document the financial costs—and resulting increases in student tuitions—prompted by college and university's efforts to achieve sustainability—now in excess of $3.4 billion per year, accompanied by a growing call to divest in carbon-based fuel stocks.[20]

SUMMING UP

Engaging with students in the dorms and on campuses can enhance the college experience. But it can also do quite the opposite. Consider whether it might be better for your son or daughter to live off campus—particularly if the school your child ends up attending is on the "party school" list. Learn whether living on campus is optional or required for freshmen.

On the other hand, there are many freshmen who are well equipped to live alone or to find an off-campus roommate before they enroll. You will want to have an honest conversation with your child to decide what makes sense for you.

Chapter 6

Get the Facts on Drinking, Socializing, and Campus Culture

It doesn't take a college degree to know that drinking and substance abuse are rampant on our college campuses. The stories of binge drinking and tragic consequences of students who engaged in excessive consumption are regularly in the news—making engaged parenting in this area especially important. Yes, we can all agree that alcohol has always been an element of the college social scene. But in recent years, its use has risen sharply, along with marijuana and other illegal substances.[1]

In various studies covering the years 1998–2005, it was reported that

- 1,825 college students between the ages of eighteen and twenty-four per 100,000 died from alcohol-related deaths, including automobile crashes.
- Almost 600,000 students were injured under the influence of alcohol.
- 400,000 students between the ages of eighteen and twenty-four had unprotected sex and more than 100,000 had been too intoxicated to know if they consented to having sex.[2]

The recent stories about rampant rape and sexual assault on campus may well be exaggerated.[3] But one thing is surely true—sexual assault and other impermissible behaviors do occur. And they do not occur in a vacuum. For too many students, the experience on campus has become four years (or six!) of partying and drinking—rather than a time of academic growth and character development. What ever happened to serious studying and learning?

No parent wants his or her child's time at college undermined by too many parties, or worse, to lose his or her child to binge drinking and its consequences. So what's a parent to do?

Check out the party school ratings. The *Princeton Review* every year issues a ranking and, while surely not definitive, it will give you some insight into the perceived culture on campus.[4] You may want to think twice about those colleges.

Check out the Clery Act reports. Federal law requires colleges and universities to report, on an annual basis, the frequency of drug- and alcohol-related incidents that occur on their campuses. You can find them by accessing the Campus Safety and Security Data Analysis Cutting Tool, a user-friendly Department of Education resource.[5] Since reporting is limited to events that result in disciplinary action or arrest, these reports do not tell the full story—but they will shed some light on what happens on campuses.

What allows for a party culture? A broken academic culture and a lack of academic demands. The National Survey of Student Engagement (NSSE) every year analyzes the study habits and lifestyles of students on campus. In one recent survey, NSSE found that 38 percent of college seniors spent ten hours per week or less preparing for classes, while 58 percent spent fifteen hours or less. In other words, most students studied no more than two hours per day—and many don't even do that. In its 2015 survey, barely more than half (54 percent) of first-year students and only 61 percent of senior students said they were highly challenged by their classes to do their best work.[6]

Adding class time and study time together, we find that most students are spending substantially fewer hours per week on academic tasks than the hours required for a normal nine-to-five job. Because these students have a

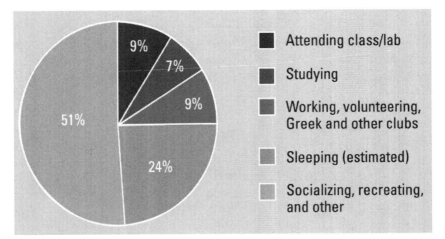

Figure 6.1. Student Time Use. *Source:* Arum, Richard, Roksa, Josipa, and Cho, Esther, *Improving Undergraduate Learning: Findings and Policy Recommendations from the SSRC-CLA Longitudinal Project,* Figure 2, https://www.saddleback.edu/uploads/la/documents/SSRCImprovingUndergraduateLearning.pdf.

great deal of free time, it is not unusual for the weekend to start on Thursday night and continue through Sunday. Needless to say, time spent partying cuts directly into time that could be spent studying. According to a survey of over 30,000 freshmen on seventy-six campuses, "students who consumed at least one drink in the last two weeks spent an average of 10.2 hours a week drinking, versus an average of 8.4 hours a week studying."[7]

So when you look at schools, find out whether there is a full roster of courses on Fridays. Since workdays in the real world start at 8:00 or 9:00 AM, find out also how many classes meet at 8:00 or 9:00 AM. It's part of career preparation, whether or not students and professors like it. If you are looking at a public institution and can't find this data, go to your legislator (or the university board) and insist that they be made available.

Find out about grades on campus, and by specific program, if possible. Within the same school, some departments will be distinguished by high standards, others not. The sad fact is that rampant grade inflation has made partying a whole lot easier. A 2012 study by Stuart Rojstaczer and Christopher Healy found that, as of 2009, "A's represent 43% of all letter grades, an increase of 28 percentage points since 1960 and 12 percentage points since 1988."[8] An academic environment that gives positive reinforcement for half-hearted efforts and substandard work is not a learning environment.

SUMMING UP

There is no reason students shouldn't have fun in college. But fun shouldn't come at the expense of a rigorous and serious academic experience. As outlined in this chapter, too many colleges today are asking little of students academically and are fostering a party culture that allows minimal academic effort. As you explore college choices, be sure to assess whether schools on your list are putting studying and learning first.

Chapter 7

Put a Premium on Free Speech

Back in December 1820, as he founded the University of Virginia, Thomas Jefferson laid out the foundation of academic freedom. "[The University] will be based on the illimitable freedom of the human mind," he wrote. "For here we are not afraid to follow truth wherever it may lead, nor to tolerate any error so long as reason is left free to combat it."[1]

For many years, there was fairly uniform agreement: Nothing is more central to the life of the mind than academic freedom—the robust exchange of ideas. In an eloquent statement dating back to 1915, the American Association of University Professors explicitly outlined the faculty freedom to teach and the student freedom to learn.[2]

Yet, over the past fifty years, there has been growing disagreement about what freedom to teach and freedom to learn actually mean. Concerned that many students—especially minority—did not feel free to learn on the college campus, schools began to take steps to ensure sensitivity and civility. Various codes have proliferated on campus outlining what kinds of behavior and comments are acceptable and what are not. These codes are typically called antiharassment policies; antibullying policies; policies on tolerance, respect, and civility; policies on bias and hate speech; and policies governing speakers, demonstrations, and rallies.

But, as in so many things, good intentions may have unintended consequences. And the advent of these codes is surely one of those times. While some codes properly enforce dangerous or indefensible behavior, too many go far afield—intruding on free speech, academic freedom, and free expression. The enforcers of sensitivity and civility codes—more accurately called *speech codes*—typically have extensive power to discipline and punish those who transgress them. So what starts out intended to foster civility or to prohibit illegal harassment, becomes, in the hands of administrators, a power-ful weapon that, in too many cases, is used to shut down politically unpopular or disfavored opinions—all in pursuit of making students feel comfortable or "safe"—hence the term *safe space.*

As Jefferson saw it—and most parents should too—a university is *not* a safe space. Of course, students should at all times be safe from physical harm. But protecting students from physical harm is not the same as protect-ing students from learning about and addressing challenging, unorthodox, or even erroneous ideas. The goal of a university is not to make people feel comfortable in what they already believe or to give administrators the power to dictate what is acceptable, but to give students the tools and the "freedom" to examine controversial matters from all sides in order to make up their own mind.

But, sadly, the notions of truth and objectivity—the necessary conditions of academic freedom outlined by Jefferson—are now regarded by many as old-fashioned and obstacles to social change. And, in the name of civility and sensitivity, expression of thoughts on race, gender, sexual orientation, and other hot-button contemporary topics is often off-limits. When that happens, the university becomes a place of indoctrination rather than education—what many refer to as the *politically correct university.*

As Greg Lukianoff, president and CEO of the Foundation for Individual Rights in Education (FIRE), has explained "administrators [on campus] have been able to convince well-meaning students to accept outright cen-sorship by creating the impression that freedom of speech is somehow the enemy of social progress. When students began leaving college with that lesson under their belts, it was only a matter of time before the cultivation of bad intellectual habits on campus started harming the dialogue of our entire country."[3]

Each year, FIRE issues a report, *Spotlight on Speech Codes: The State of Free Speech on Our Nation's Campuses.* In 2016, FIRE surveyed over 400 schools and found that 49.3 percent maintained severely restrictive "red light" speech codes—defined as "policies that clearly and substantially prohibit protected speech."[4]

For our purposes, we'll look at just one, this one at Colby College, which was named FIRE's "Speech Code of the Month" in July 2016.[5] In it, Colby proclaimed that "unwelcome hostile or intimidating remarks, spoken or writ-ten[,] . . . or physical gestures" constitute harassment that can be reported to Colby's bias response team. Looking at that very broad language, almost anything could be construed as "unwelcome," "hostile," or "intimidating." And, based on the bias response log, it turns out "almost anything" was. For example, one complaint read, "At a Halloween party, a student reported seeing three students wearing a sombrero, poncho, and mustache as costumes." After FIRE drew attention to the log, Colby changed its settings to require a password for access, perhaps realizing how ludicrous the targeted incidents—and attention to them—appeared.[6]

Colby is not alone: At many colleges, what was once innocent can now be seen as cause for litigation. Take personal relationships: Little did we realize—in those dating days long ago—that an awkward date or misinterpreted facial expression could have long-lasting consequences. Young men (and young women) are now at risk of being accused of sexual harassment or even sexual assault—and prosecuted on campus by tribunals that need not apply due process—if they simply engage in sexual jokes, inappropriate laughter, and unwanted flirtation.[7]

Trigger Warnings

And there's more: The idea of triggering was conceived by psychiatrists after World War I, when many soldiers returned with post-traumatic stress disorder–like symptoms. The warnings were to limit painful flashbacks and panic attacks. But trigger warnings have now become a regular feature of curricular offerings.[8]

Student leaders at the University of California–Santa Barbara passed a resolution urging university officials to institute mandatory trigger warnings on class syllabi. Professors who offer "content that may trigger the onset of symptoms of Post-Traumatic Stress Disorder" would be required not only to issue advance alerts but also to permit students to skip those classes during which the content at issue is covered.[9]

Microaggressions

Trigger warnings are bad enough, but there is an even more troubling development when it comes to free speech: the "microaggression." Microaggressions are generally innocuous questions or statements that become grounds for punishment of students and faculty because of perceived offense. In recent months, the number of perceived offenses has grown exponentially. In California, for example, administrators issued a list of statements that would be deemed microaggressions—comments such as those suggesting that "America is the land of opportunity," that "the most qualified person should get the job," and that "gender plays no part in who [*sic*] we hire."[10] At Oberlin, taking offense took on new dimensions when the students complained that the poor preparation of ethnic food by dining hall workers was "appropriative" and racist.[11] This is not just ridiculous; it is a dangerous assault on free speech.

> - America is the land of opportunity.
> - I believe the most qualified person should get the job.
> - Being forced to choose "Male" or "Female" when completing basic forms.

Figure 7.1.   Examples of Microaggressions. *Source:* **UCLA diversity guidance.**

"Disinvitations"

Choosing a campus speaker used to be about hearing from a distinguished person, often someone who had taken a controversial stance. But not anymore.

On many campuses, students and faculty now are often less interested in hearing a challenging perspective than they are in what one college president has called "freedom from unpalatable speech—or more typically, what is perceived to be distasteful by a few."[12] This is the sadly widespread practice of "disinviting" speakers because some students or faculty don't like what the speakers have to say.

Brandeis University invited human rights activist Ayaan Hirsi Ali to speak and receive an honorary degree—and then rescinded the invitation because of student protests.[13] Former secretary of state Condoleezza Rice felt the pressure to bow out of speaking at Rutgers after students protested she was a war criminal; their behavior was so outrageous that it later drew the condemnation of President Obama.[14]

Azusa Pacific University invited scholar Charles Murray to give a talk (not even a commencement address) and then backed out because Murray, an eminent American social scientist, was deemed too controversial.[15]

Christine Lagarde, the first female head of the International Monetary Fund, was invited to address Smith's graduating class only to back out after students protested her support of what they considered imperialist and patriarchal systems.[16]

We all know: Sensitivity to others, fostering friendship, solidarity, harmony, and civility are important—and our children should surely understand the importance of those values. But, in the words of Yale's seminal Woodward Report, if we make "the fostering of friendship, solidarity, harmony, civility or mutual respect" the "primary and dominant value" on campus, then we risk "sacrificing [the university's] central purpose," teaching and scholarship.[17]

The rapid growth of this "offense-sensitive" culture on college campuses undermines the very purpose of our educational institutions—to follow truth

Figure 7.2. Disinvitations. *Source*: Christine Lagarde, World Economic Forum, commons.wikimedia; Condoleezza Rice and John Derbyshire, public domain; Suzanne Venker, twitter.com/suzannevenker; Charles Murray and Ayaan Hirsi Ali, Gage Skidmore, commons. wikimedia.

wherever it may lead and to engage in a robust conversation about controversial issues of the day.

As a parent, you should look with alarm at a school that has a "red light" speech code or that welcomes trigger warnings and microaggressions. Schools that put sensitivities first are losing sight of their educational mission. And if your child is an independent thinker, he or she may find such an environment stifling and oppressive.

To get a better idea of which schools do this and which don't, take a look at *What Will They Learn?* website, www.whatwilltheylearn.com. The website includes information on speech codes compiled by the Foundation for Individual Rights in Education. A red stop light or yellow caution light means the school has adopted regulations that restrict speech protected by the Constitution and the norms of academic freedom. Think twice about any school that restricts speech in this way.

At the very least, express your displeasure and publicly ask the school why it chooses to do so.

Chapter 8

Aim for Four Years and Out

What ever happened to the four-year college degree? That's another question well worth asking. In times gone by, the college trajectory was clear—four years and out.

But my, how things have changed! Six years is now the norm used by the U.S. Department of Education for graduation, making many schools appear more successful than they are.

The most recent data from the U.S. Department of Education show that only about 40 percent of first-time, full-time students earn a degree in four years. A still paltry 59.4 percent of first-time, full-time students even earn a bachelor's degree in six years from the school where they started.[1]

This is not a good trend.

The more expensive privates, it turns out, do better than the publics when it comes to graduation, with four-year rates of roughly 53 percent compared to 34 percent in the publics.[2]

It's true. The data are imperfect given widespread college transfers which are not captured in the numbers. But the fact remains: these graduation rates are too low, especially when compared to global competitors. Our results look particularly bad when we consider that we spend 79 percent more on full-time students than the average for peer countries, but still rank nineteenth—yes, nineteenth—in the percentage of adults who have completed college.[3]

The longer a student goes to college, the greater the financial costs—and opportunity costs as well. And for students who don't graduate, the consequences can be tragic.

The adjoining charts show the four-year graduation rates of the top-ranked national colleges and universities in the country.

	4-Year Graduation Rate	
INSTITUTION	Class of 2008	Class of 2013
University of California–Berkeley	69.0%	73.0%
University of California–Los Angeles	68.0	74.0
University of Virginia	85.0	87.0
University of Michigan	72.0	75.0
University of North Carolina	75.0	81.0
College of William & Mary	82.0	82.0
Georgia Institute of Technology	33.0	40.0
University of California–Santa Barbara	64.0	68.0
University of California–Irvine	60.0	72.0
University of California–San Diego	57.0	58.0
University of California–Davis	51.0	58.0
University of Illinois–Urbana-Champaign	67.0	71.0
University of Wisconsin–Madison	50.0	56.0
Pennsylvania State University	62.0	64.0
University of Florida	59.0	66.0
Ohio State University	49.0	59.0
University of Texas	53.0	52.0
University of Washington	54.0	63.0
University of Connecticut	66.0	70.0
University of Maryland	62.0	69.0
Clemson University	50.0	58.0
Purdue University–West Lafayette	38.0	47.0
University of Georgia	52.0	62.0
University of Pittsburgh	61.0	64.0
University of Minnesota	46.0	59.0
Texas A&M University	46.0	51.0
Virginia Polytechnic Institute and State University	53.0	62.0
Rutgers University	53.0	58.0
Colorado School of Mines	38.0	49.0
Indiana University	50.0	60.0
Michigan State University	48.0	51.0
University of Delaware	62.0	65.0
University of Massachusetts	52.0	66.0

Figure 8.1. Baccalaureate Graduation Rates for First-Time, Full-Time Freshmen. *U.S. News & World Report* Top 50 National Universities.

Miami University	68.0	65.0
University of California–Santa Cruz	50.0	55.0
University of Iowa	44.0	51.0
State University of New York-State University of New York–Binghamton University	63.0	69.0
North Carolina State University	41.0	44.0
State University of New York-Stony Brook University	43.0	47.0
State University of New York-College of Environmental Science and Forestry	41.0	59.0
University of Colorado	41.0	47.0
University of Vermont	61.0	66.0
Florida State University	50.0	62.0
University of Alabama	38.0	41.0
State University of New York-University at Buffalo	43.0	55.0
Auburn University	36.0	44.0
University of Missouri	43.0	46.0
University of Nebraska	29.0	33.0
University of New Hampshire	56.0	63.0
University of Oregon	44.0	50.0
University of Tennessee	31.0	43.0

Source: Integrated Postsecondary Education Data System.

Note: Original data were reported without decimal points. "Class of 2008" and "Class of 2013" refer to the cohorts of first-time, full-time freshmen who entered in 2004 and 2009.

Figure 8.1.   Continued

You should have these in hand when you visit these colleges. Or go to www.whatwilltheylearn.com, which provides four-year grad rates, or College Navigator's website, www.nces.ed.gov/collegenavigator/, a helpful website of the National Center for Education Statistics that will give you lots of information to help you understand the real costs of the schools you are examining.

While there is no single reason for low graduation rates, they often point to weak advising, a destructive party culture, or poor scheduling of classes. If the numbers are bad, in single digits or low double digits, you should listen to the warning bells and look at another school.

And what about retention rates? What exactly do they mean, and do they represent a metric worth worrying about? First-year retention rates for first-time full-time students measure the percentage of students who continue the following year as sophomores. Stated another way, this is the first-year dropout rate.

This figure is important because remaining after the first year is a good predictor that the student will complete his or her degree. If there is a high dropout rate, it can also indicate that the admissions office has failed to admit students who are adequately prepared academically or socially. At the same time, don't place *too* much reliance on this figure! Sadly, because schools want to have good numbers and keep students at the school, some are more interested in a form of higher ed "social promotion" than they are in truly reflecting the student's ability to succeed.[4]

Be cautious when considering programs abroad. More and more colleges are encouraging students to study abroad and to undertake academic programs off campus—and that's all to the good, mostly. There are, however, stories about students who discover—after it's too late—that the courses they took won't transfer for credit.[5] They then have to take additional courses to make up for what they did abroad, extending their graduation date well past those of their classmates. Time is money, so don't let this happen.

And ask tough questions when it comes to graduation rates and affordability.

Purdue University recently produced a "College Planning Checklist" that includes a number of terrific questions along these lines.[6] These include:

- How much has your total cost of attendance risen in the past year?
- What is the average debt of your students who borrow?
- What is the average starting salary of graduates in the major in which I'm interested?
- Do you plan a tuition freeze?
- Do you have a guaranteed tuition rate for four years so I'll know the costs for my college career?
- What is the four-year graduation rate for my major? Average time to degree?
- How does the institution facilitate students graduating in four years?
- What are your total costs—tuition, room and board, books and other expenses?
- Are there differential fees for majors?

As Purdue recognizes: "Many colleges and universities could be a great educational fit for you, but financial fit and return on your investment are fundamental to college choice."[7]

TAKE A GAP YEAR?

There is no harm in students being undecided on a major when entering, so long as they are able to complete bachelor's degrees in four years. One of the reasons students take so long is they often change majors and thus stay in school longer to meet requirements.

If educational and career goals are unclear, it may be quite beneficial for your child to delay entering college for a year. There are many excellent gap programs that give students an opportunity to think through what they want in college—and life. And there is always the option of taking a job in your home community. Your child should also feel free to take a leave of absence—once in college—to work and clarify personal and professional goals.

In some states, we have seen legislatures starting to tackle the issue of low four-year graduation rates. For example, in 2009, the Florida state legislature passed a law establishing an "Excess Credit Hour Surcharge" for credit hours above those required for a baccalaureate degree. As of fall 2015, thousands of students were still taking significantly more courses than required, but the recent law is a constructive development.[8]

SUMMING UP

Finishing efficiently should be a priority for any student. That's why it's important to look at the graduation rates for schools you are interested in and to be very deliberate in selecting a course load that will ensure your child graduates in four years.

Chapter 9

Learn the Real Cost

Dr. Richard Vedder, distinguished professor of economics emeritus, Ohio University

The cost of a college education has been skyrocketing for decades. College tuition and required fees at four-year institutions now amount to 27 percent of the median family income.[1] And students are graduating with significant debt. Recent data from the Federal Reserve Bank of New York show that 18.5 percent of student borrowers owe between $25,001 and $50,000, and more than 4 percent owe more than $100,000![2] Nationally, the delinquency rate of all students receiving federal financial aid is nearly 20 percent, while almost seven million are in default entirely.[3] The reports are frequent and clear.

Despite this disturbing news, too many families still allow themselves to get swept up in events instead of planning ahead. Too often, they are persuaded that college debt is "good debt." Too often, they have little idea of what they will pay or how they will finance their children's education until the final decision must be made. This is not a good story.

So, again, what's a parent to do?

The first question to ask and answer is: What is the real cost?

STICKER VS. NET PRICE

Except for buying a house, paying for college is the biggest spending item in the lifetime of most families, and those costs have risen rather dramatically over time.[4] Making things even worse, it is often very hard to calculate—accurately and quickly—what it will cost for your child to attend a college.

When it comes to buying a new car, we all know there's a difference between the sticker price and the real price. The same thing is true in higher education. But with college, the sticker price—the price advertised on the

"I have not calculated
how much your diplomas
cost in time and money.
Whatever those ballpark
figures are, they surely
deserve this reaction from
me today: Wow. Wow.
Wow."

—Kurt Vonnegut, 2001
speech at Rice University

Figure 9.1.   *Source:* Kurt Vonnegut, 2001, speech at Rice University.

website for tuition and fees, and room and board—is usually a good deal more than what a typical student pays. Full sticker price is *not* the net price paid by students who receive institutional or federal financial aid. Moreover, the difference in price between public and private schools is often a good deal less than what sticker prices suggest.

Let's explain. A majority of students at American colleges and universities get some financial aid, often given by the school itself. At most schools, well under half the students pay the sticker price. Indeed, studies show that there is as much as a 56 percent differential when it comes to the sticker price and the net cost.[5] The basic charges for tuition, room, and food are discounted—most students pay less than the stated amount.

Still, the sticker price has meaning—for perhaps roughly 30–40 percent of students, the sticker price is the amount they are *required* to pay, and they know when they apply that basic college costs will not *exceed* that amount, at least for their first year.[6]

You can produce an estimate of your family's net cost of attendance at a given school with the help of the school's net-price calculator. In 2008, Congress mandated that colleges and universities post a net-price calculator on their websites so that students could estimate the likely cost of college after grant aid.[7] Every school has one. Use it!

The Department of Education also has a College Scorecard (collegescorecard.ed.gov) designed to help students compare and contrast institutions on key metrics, including costs, graduation rate, median borrowing, loan default rate, and salary outcomes. It can be a very valuable resource, especially when coupled with Big Future (bigfuture.collegeboard.org), the online web resource made available by the College Board.

The actual cost you will pay is based to a considerable extent on financial need, and that, in turn, is usually determined by information provided on the Free Application for Federal Student Aid (FAFSA) form, which is discussed later in the chapter, and sometimes even other data the school requests.

Sometimes there are discounts because the student has characteristics the school desires—extraordinary potential academic achievement, special talent in athletics or other skills, or racial or gender traits that the school particularly values. Faced with research showing few applications from high-achieving, low-income students, many of the so-called elite schools have taken extra steps to reach out and assure them that price is not an obstacle.[8]

Schools like Princeton, Harvard, and Yale have eliminated loans in large part from their financial aid packages. For wealthy and highly competitive schools like these, relatively low-income students get a 100 percent discount—and sometimes a formula is used that significantly discounts the net price for those students from even moderately affluent families, even $100,000 or more a year.[9] Paradoxically, sometimes it is less expensive for low-income students to attend a private college or university with a big sticker price than a state university.

Can you negotiate over the amount of discount, just as you would haggle over the price of a house or car? Sometimes—it is often worth a try. Private schools that are not extremely selective often have a hard time meeting enrollment goals, so they may be receptive to a counter-offer.[10] Nationwide, private colleges discount sticker prices more than 40 percent, on average.[11]

Suppose the tuition, room, and board charges are $45,000 a year, and the school offers Johnny a $10,000 discount (making the amount to be paid $35,000). If the school is desperate for students, there is a chance the counter-offer will be accepted: You tell the financial aid/admissions folks that "Johnny has been accepted at other roughly comparable schools that are cheaper than yours, so he cannot accept your offer unless you offer him at least an $18,000 discount from the listed fees." It doesn't hurt to ask—the worst thing that the school could say is "no."

If the college is highly competitive with lots of good applicants, your bargaining power is reduced—very often to zero. Public schools, with lower initial sticker prices and fewer private resources to finance discounting, are also less likely to bargain over price.

Two more points on fees. First, students and their parents typically assume they will pay those fees for four years. Over half the time, however, that is not the case. As noted earlier, at a typical public school, a wide majority of students take more than four years to graduate.[12]

A school with a $20,000 net (after scholarships) tuition where most students graduate in four years may actually be cheaper than one with a net tuition of $18,000 but where most students take five years to graduate. Beware of schools that charge extra tuition for students wanting to take a heavy (say 18 hour) course load in order to graduate early or just on-time. And *be sure that the school will renew scholarships (tuition discounts) for the second, third, and fourth years if the student is in good academic standing.*

And remember: The four-year graduation rate is higher at private schools than public ones, and as we have seen, tuition discounting is greater, so *the tuition price differential between private and public schools is generally overstated by just looking at sticker prices*—don't rule out private schools automatically.[13]

Second, a small but growing number of schools are offering some form of a guaranteed tuition plan. Under one model, the school guarantees that the first year sticker price will not rise through the next four years (see Figure 9.4).[14] A school with a slightly higher price initially but with a guaranteed plan might cost less over the college career than a school without such a plan.

PAYING FOR COLLEGE

How are you going to pay for college? We know of seven ways: funds provided by family or friends, scholarships that are either college-provided or given by some outside organization, federal tuition tax credits, Pell Grants, federal subsidized or unsubsidized student loans, private loans, and college and summertime employment (some of it under the Federal Work-Study Program). Family financing is usually not enough: Most families do not have, or cannot save over the next few years, the $100,000 or even $200,000 or more that it takes to finance college.[15]

Therefore, most students today receive some form of federal student financial assistance. Before you can even get a dollar of that aid (excepting federal tuition tax credits), however, you must complete the FAFSA form. The FAFSA is ten pages of 9-point type![16] You can download the form online (at http://www.fafsa.ed.gov).

Like the form, the entire government student financial assistance program is extremely complicated—instead of one or two forms, there are many. Several private companies offer assistance (for a price) to help you navigate the process, and college financial aid offices can be helpful, as well as knowledgeable high school guidance counselors.

Now let's review the major forms of federal financial assistance together.

Pell Grants do not have to be repaid—they are like scholarships and are good at any accredited school. They are targeted for low-income households—although some kids from households with over $60,000 income get these grants.[17] The size of the grant varies with need, but it never exceeds $5,730 a year at the time of writing.[18] The grants are, however, renewable for many years, so some students ultimately receive $25,000 or more in Pell financing. College financial aid offices are responsible for disbursing Pell Grant awards to eligible students.[19]

Federal Tuition Tax Credits similarly do not need to be repaid—they actually work to lower the income tax liabilities of parents of students. They are equivalent to grants, total $2,000 to $2,500 a year, and are extremely popular. This is a form of aid that moderately well-off persons can benefit from. Internal Revenue Service publication 970, *Tax Benefits for Education*, gives added information.[20]

Vastly more important than either Pell Grants or tuition credits, however, are federal student loans—Americans today owe well over one trillion dollars on such loans more than they do on credit cards or cars.[21] There are actually several different kinds of federal loans (more complications!).

Very important are federal *Stafford subsidized direct loans* administered through the U.S. Department of Education. Students generally do not have to pay any interest on the funds until six months after graduation. Interest rates are relatively low, and are now mostly tied to rates prevailing in money markets.

Eligibility for these loans is usually provided by the financial aid office of the school the student wishes to attend. *Stafford unsubsidized direct loans* are somewhat less attractive, but do not depend on financial need. Unsubsidized loans have similar interest rates as subsidized loans, but they accrue interest from the beginning, even while students are in school.[22]

If that is not complicated enough, there are a couple of other major loan possibilities—and several smaller ones for specialized training (e.g., Federal Nursing Loans).[23] *Direct PLUS loans* are made to graduate and professional students and to the *parents* of undergraduate students. The loans can be rather large—up to the "cost of attendance" at the student's school, and repayment can be deferred until six months after graduation.[24] A word of caution against undue reliance on parent PLUS loans is included in the advice offered at the end of the chapter.

Finally, there is something called *federal Perkins loans* (although some in Congress are pushing for their elimination). They are designed for those with "exceptional" financial need, and are made payable through the school, although some schools do not participate in the program.[25]

There are still other ways of financing college. An old program is *Federal Work-Study* in which some college students are provided with jobs by the college they attend, receiving usually the federal minimum wage for their efforts. Some students can make between $3,000 and $4,000 annually toward their college costs.[26]

And some students borrow money completely privately. Private loans reached almost 15 percent of all college lending in the last decade but declined to 6 percent more recently.[27] These loans avoid all the hassles with federal borrowing (you may even be able to avoid filling out the hated FAFSA form), but at a real cost: Interest rates tend to be somewhat higher, and loan terms are rigid. Almost always a parent may be required to cosign the loan: if the student fails to repay, the parent is responsible for the debt.[28]

If you are going to a relatively low-cost college, and/or if your family can meet most of the expenses, you may be able largely to finance college the old-fashioned way: family savings and working your way through school. Between employment during school and a good summer job, most students can pay at least $5,000 annually ($20,000 over four years) toward college costs and perhaps avoid the hassles of the FAFSA form and the worries about paying off college debt.

Also, new forms of college financing are beginning to evolve, such as "income share agreements," whereby students forego a share of earnings for a fixed number of years after graduation in return for partial or full payment of college expenses.[29] Even with federal student loans, the government has initiated a series of repayment plans tied to earnings after graduation, and some students with low earnings after graduation ultimately will have some of their loans forgiven.[30]

Consider a 529 Plan. In recent years, 529 plans have survived efforts to eliminate them. 529 plans provide families protection against tuition. These 529 plans are offered by all fifty states and the District of Columbia, and you can shop around because you need not participate in your own state's plan. About a dozen states also offer prepaid tuition plans.[31]

Since these savings plans are not counted as a family asset, grandparents can also contribute and thereby reduce their estates, without gift tax penalties.[32] A lawyer or financial planner can provide important details.

HOW MUCH DEBT?

How much debt should students incur? Unfortunately, there is not a single magic number. Under federal law, schools are required to provide information to students about the debt they assume.[33] But it's still a tough calculation. The capacity of students to repay loans depends not only on the amount borrowed but also on earnings after college. You can go to Payscale.com to see the median starting salaries of the schools you are considering.

The New York Times

Placing the Blame as Students Are Buried in Debt

- Cortney Munna
  Major: Feminist Studies

- Owed $100,000

- After graduation, hired as
  a photographer's assistant

Cortney Munna hoped for the best when she decided to attend New York University. Now she owes $100,000.

Figure 9.2. *Source:* **Photo from** *The New York Times,* **May 29 © 2010.** *The New York Times.* **All rights reserved. Used by permission and protected by the Copyright Laws of the United States. The printing, copying, redistribution, or retransmission of this Content without express written permission is prohibited.**

True, amounts to be borrowed and earned cannot be perfectly predicted in advance. (How do you know even if your child is going to graduate in four years, for example?) Still, weighing the potential debt against potential earnings should be a definite check-off for families searching for the right college.

An old rule of thumb was that students probably should not incur debt equal to much more than one year's postgraduation earnings, which for most students would be somewhere below $50,000.[34] The possibility of loan forgiveness on income-based repayment plans might modify that a bit, but incurring more than $50,000 in debt for undergraduate school would seem imprudent.

Students tend to be overly optimistic. They often assume they will graduate in four years, yet a majority don't. They assume they will get a good job right after graduation, one paying minimally $40,000 a year and maybe a good bit more and that they will thereafter soon be promoted and make even more.[35]

The majority of recent college graduates are either unemployed or underemployed, working relatively low-paying jobs often filled by high school graduates. It is hard to repay large student loans on the earnings of a barista, taxi cab driver, or unskilled construction worker. No wonder reports indicate large portions of recent graduates still live with their parents and are getting financial assistance from them.[36]

"Young Adults, Student Debt and Economic Well-Being"

About 40% of all households headed by adults under 40 now have some level of student debt—the median amount of $13,000—according to the Pew study. That's the highest proportion in history.

Student Debtors Carry a Heavier Overall Debt Load
Median total indebtedness of young households

COLLEGE EDUCATED

Has student debt — $137,010

No student debt — $73,250

NOT COLLEGE EDUCATED

Has student debt — $28,300

No student debt — $2,500

Note: Total indebtedness includes all types of debt: mortgage debt, vehicle loans, credit cards, other debt, as well as student debt. Young households are households with heads younger than 40. Households are characterized based on the educational attainment of the household head. "College educated" refers to those with a bachelor's degree or more. Student debtor households have outstanding student loan balances or student loans in deferment.

Source: Pew Research Center tabulations of the 2010 Survey of Consumer Finances

PEW RESEARCH CENTER

"Young Adults, Student Debt and Economic Well-Being," Pew Research Center, Washington, DC (May 2014) http://www.pewsocialtrends.org/2014/05/14/young-adults-student-debt-and-economic-well-being/

Figure 9.3. *Source:* Richard Fry, "Young Adults, Student Debt and Economic Well-Being," Pew Research Center, Washington, DC (May 2014), http://www.pewsocialtrends.org/2014/05/14/young-adults-student-debt-and-economic-well-being/.

BE HONEST ABOUT FAMILY FINANCES

How much can a family really afford to pay without shouldering burdensome debt? This question may sound simple, but to answer it, family members need to be honest with themselves and each other.

On the one side, students have their ideas about what they want. Selecting a list of "finalists" is almost an inevitable ritual when it comes to the college application process.

On the other side, there are financial realities for families and unsettling trends in higher education that families need to face.

Federally backed parental debt totals $100 billion.[37] And this has been exacerbated by the availability of the parent PLUS loan, with an interest rate of 6.31 percent.[38] No less a figure than former presidential candidate and Maryland governor Martin O'Malley knows the "price" of PLUS loans. Responding to his children's desire to go to colleges out of state, the O'Malley family accumulated a crushing debt—$339,200 in student loans through the PLUS loans program.[39] Parents, don't do it.

A Sampling of Schools and Systems That Have Frozen or Cut Tuition
LaSalle University, Philadelphia, PA
Otterbein University, Westerville, OH
Purdue University, West Lafayette, IN
Rosemont College, Rosemont, PA
University of Illinois System
University of Maine System
University of Missouri System
University of North Carolina System
University of Washington, Seattle, WA
University System of Georgia
Utica College, Utica, NY

A Sampling of Schools with Three-Year Degree Programs
American University, Washington, DC
Ashland University, Ashland, OH
Austin Peay State University, Clarksville, TN
Ball State University, Muncie, IN
Bates College, Lewiston, ME
Florida State University, Tallahassee, FL
Hartwick College, Oneonta, NY
Lake Forest College, Lake Forest, IL
Mississippi State University, Mississippi State, MS
Mount St. Mary's University, Emmitsburg, MD
The Ohio State University, Columbus, OH
Southern Oregon University, Ashland, OR
University of Iowa, Iowa City, IA
University of San Francisco, San Francisco, CA
Wesleyan University, Middletown, CT

A Sampling of Schools with Four-Year Degree Guarantees
Baylor University, Waco, TX
Belmont Abbey College, Belmont, NC
George Washington University, Washington, DC
Miami University, Oxford, OH
Ohio University, Athens, OH
Portland State University, Portland, OR
Randolph-Macon College, Ashland, VA
Sewanee-University of the South, Sewanee, TN
SUNY-University at Buffalo, Buffalo, NY
Texas A&M University, College Station, TX
University of Arizona, Tucson, AZ
University of Illinois–Urbana-Champaign, Urbana, IL
University of Oklahoma, Norman, OK
University of Virginia, Charlottesville, VA
University of Texas–Austin, Austin, TX

Note: For public schools that have cut or frozen tuition, the freeze sometimes applies only for in-state students. There are two common types of four-year degree guarantees: one that freezes tuition at the starting price for four years and one in which the school promises with stipulations to pay for remaining coursework if the student is unable to graduate within four years.

Figure 9.4. A Sampling of Schools and Systems.

Be cautious and realistic. Learn what the discounted price of a school will be, what the probability is that your child will graduate in four years, and what earnings are for the planned major—knowing he or she may not equal the typical student. Expensive colleges often have a higher percentage of graduates who make good earnings. Remember sticker prices, while not meaningless, are not the best indicator of college costs.

SUMMING UP

Yes, it's true: The college decision is an important one and students should be involved from the get-go. We know: In this special time, you don't want to let your kids down. But face reality: You'll want to weigh in early with what is reasonable financially and what is not. And saddling your child (or you!) with immense debt will not be doing anyone a favor.

Chapter 10

Visit with Your Eyes Open

If you are like most families, you'll plan a trip to your "wish list" schools during spring break of your child's junior year. You'll likely know when tours occur and have carefully scheduled your visit to coincide. You'll be prompt in arriving at the admissions center to meet good-looking "student ambassadors," who volunteer expressly for the job, or are paid by the university, to take you and your children on a tour designed to make you decide this place is "the one."

Of course, tours vary, but they can be counted on to showcase the dorms, athletic facilities, and experiences on campus. Most schools will talk a bit about academics—indeed, at Columbia University in New York City, students impressively and cogently outline the value of a core curriculum.[1] But more likely, the tours and the discussions will focus less on academic expectations, and more on advising, dorm food, social life, and other campus activities. If your child is an athlete, you'll probably get a special tour of the athletic facilities and maybe a visit from the team captain as well.

Enjoy the tour and listen closely. If the tour guide barely mentions academics, take note. As you walk on campus, take a look at other students: Are they talking, texting, or debating? Do they look intense, sad, or happy? Look at the flyers advertising campus events. What kind of social and cultural activities do they describe?

Try to learn more than what is mentioned on the canned tour. Find out what students are studying and how much reading and writing they do. Does the tour guide meet with an advisor once a month, once a term, or rarely? Is he or she required to consult with faculty about course requirements? Have they ever talked about a course with a faculty member outside of class? These are the kinds of questions that may make students—and institutions—rethink what parental and student priorities should be.

And do visit classroom buildings and actual classes. Schools will often have a ready-made list of courses where faculty know that prospective students and parents may be in the audience. But don't be shy. Try them out and visit as many courses as you can—and talk to the professors. If the institution has only provided a small list, ask if you can visit others as well; you may have a particular class or department in mind. Even if you don't enter the class, peek in through the windows and watch the professor-student interaction.

CHECK OUT THE STUDENTS

Chat with a few in the hallway. And check out the library too: are many students there and what are they doing?

Also, visit the college bookstore or bookstores. This can often be a treasure trove of insights into the university and its priorities. Take a look at what is for sale, trinkets and otherwise. Find course listings and look at the books that are on the reading list, just as enrolled students do. Do they suggest courses that are rigorous and challenging? Or are the readings quirky and narrow in scope?

Be aware, too, that professors may use alternatives. At the University of Pennsylvania, for example, professors have used no fewer than five vendors, and not only the official Barnes and Noble managed location.[2]

Read the school newspaper while you are there, and subscribe once you leave. Student journalists are often fearless in examining campus crimes, problems, or concerns—and papers can be one of the very best ways to get real insight into what makes a school tick.

And take a close look at other things on campus. What about campus kiosks and campus bulletin boards? They can offer a very real sense of what activities and clubs the school sponsors and what speakers are coming to town.

How about a visit to campus coffee bars and eating spots? Why not help yourself to a smoothie and listen in on conversations—or engage the students yourself. And stick around for the evening and weekend too. Is the campus quiet on Thursday night, or are students drinking and carousing? Is the campus empty on Saturday? What are the library hours on Saturday and Sunday? This kind of sleuthing can tell you a lot about the campus culture.

START THINKING ABOUT A JOB

When visiting a college, it makes sense to scout out what career services the university offers. Does it have a career services office? Are there placement initiatives and counseling? Can it provide you with a list of companies that make campus visits to identify students for their team? Are internships available—and what kind?

Some schools have developed student-alumni mentoring programs—and dig a bit to find out if such a program exists on campuses of your choice. The Edge Program at Randolph Macon College, for example, provides a "personalized, comprehensive four-year career preparation program that's integrated with the student's academic experience," including a well-attended employment-oriented boot camp.[3]

Family members and students should become familiar with economic data that will help shed light on occupation availability and incomes earned, as well as the success of individual schools and majors when it comes to finding a job. If you live in Virginia, Tennessee, Texas, Colorado, or Arkansas, you are lucky. These states have available a growing base of financial information that sheds light on the success of students graduating from institutions in their states.[4]

You may also want to look at websites that are designed to help families measure their return on investment. One such website is the College Reality Check, collegerealitycheck.com, produced by the *Chronicle of Higher Education*, which outlines net price, graduation rates, debt, default rates, and graduate earnings for the schools in the database. The reason? This kind of information can help you avoid colleges where your child is likely to drop out or you are likely to take on too much debt. As we saw in chapter 9, you want to find a college that is a good "financial fit"—balancing what you pay with your child's chance of success.

SUMMING UP

The school will give you its version of the campus. But you can come away with far more insights if you are attentive and know where to look. Visiting the bookstore, attending classes, and checking out career services can tell you a lot about a prospective campus.

REMAINING INVOLVED

Chapter 11

Stay Connected

Getting admitted is just the start of the story. Following up on the insights you gained in the selection process is equally—perhaps even more—important. The following sections outline important ways to stay connected to your college student, most especially in the first year.

LOCKING IN A GOOD COURSE SCHEDULE

Over the years, some schools have integrated parental involvement into the first-year student's experience. Even if it is not expected, it's important to be involved. Helping your child identify a broad and rigorous course load should be a number one goal. Before your child registers for each quarter or semester, take the opportunity to sit down together and talk about course plans. If possible, encourage five courses per semester—not four. This will require focus on academics and also allow your student to graduate in four years.

There is no need to declare a major immediately. Instead urge your child to use the first two years of college—and thoughtful general education courses—to explore options and broaden perspectives. It's important to explore many fields early because once a student has committed to a major, it may be impossible to change because of a lack of time or money.

While narrow and trendy subjects may be appealing, explain that broad survey courses in history, literature, math, and science are more likely to serve long-term needs, providing the knowledge and skills needed to perform effectively in the workplace and as a citizen.[1] As we learned in the first section, some schools will structure what students should know and be able to do. But most won't. So your advice is very important.

Urge your child for example, to take at least one economics survey course to understand the laws of supply and demand. Outline the importance of taking courses on Western and world civilization—and surveys on music and art. Couple these with a concentrated study of U.S. history or government, including the American Constitution and the Bill of Rights, so that he or she will know and understand the rights and responsibilities they establish.

Encourage your child to gain proficiency in foreign languages, knowing that the very best understanding of other cultures comes through their language and literature. Underscore how courses in literature and composition will help him or her thoughtfully critique what is in the news and powerfully express himself or herself. And encourage him or her to take at least one course each in college-level math and science. Make it clear that it's important for students to pursue challenging subjects, even ones they will not likely study after graduation on their own. And refer your child to Appendix A, which offers the helpful perspective of a college freshman.

Urge your child to have a range of course options—not just one set of desired classes. Often, the first choice courses are not available. So it's important to have plans B and C.

Consider a double major. And writing a thesis can also be an important and challenging experience—and achievement—that will hone research and writing skills and ensure that your child works closely with a professor.

GRADUATING IN FOUR YEARS: AN ACTION PLAN

Here's a roadmap to graduating in four years:

Identify early on how many credits are required to graduate. The typical college expects 120 credit hours or eight semesters.[2] Confirm this when you begin.

Locate various majors that are appealing and find out their requirements as well. Again, a typical department will require approximately thirty credits to graduate with a major—along with gen ed credits and electives. Some departments, such as engineering, require substantially more credits.[3] Know in advance what those are and look closely before enrolling in such a department.

Discourage Major Shifting

One of the reasons so many students take more than 120 credits is their decision to switch majors midstream, particularly after their second year of college.[4] Yes, it's true: sometimes it takes time to figure out the best path. At the end of junior year, Susie may discover that she really wanted to major in psychology, rather than history. But these switches can be very costly—and should be avoided if possible.

Pencil in a course schedule for all four years that will show you the way to a four-year degree. Ask your child to review this with his or her advisor and—if he or she isn't helpful—go to the dean of students and ask for help. Encourage your child to make sure his or her advisor understands and approves the course schedule.

PREPARING FOR ORIENTATION AND THE FIRST DAYS AT SCHOOL

In the old days, you could expect orientations to address such issues as the honor code, academic expectations, roommate conflict resolution, fire and safety guidance, alcohol policies, and security issues. But now, residential programming at many schools has become intrusive, rather than informational.

Take the University of Delaware for example: There, some years ago, students were forced to answer deeply personal questions regarding sexual identity and racial privilege—practically on their first day.[5] Hamilton College attempted, before being challenged, to require all freshman males to attend a program called "She Fears You." The program, ultimately made optional, was designed to address the proclivity—in Hamilton's view—of young men to be rapists![6]

A number of organizations blew the whistle on these coercive programs and Delaware, in particular, became the watchword for orientation indoctrination. But the stories of heavy-handed orientations are, regrettably, quite common. Students who are brand new to campus and college life certainly can't be expected to easily say no to events, meetings, and ideas pushed relentlessly by adults in charge.

Fortunately, in the days of the internet, it's hard for schools to hide their politically correct programs. Cellphones and iPhones provide an opportunity to tape and photograph what the program directors demand.

If residential programming goes beyond appropriate activities, such as study skills, and verges into intrusive and inappropriate matters of conscience, viewpoint, and belief, it's important that your son or daughter push back. What I mean are programs that require you to outline whether you are privileged, that ask you to reveal your sexual orientation, or that urge you to reject your religious beliefs.

These are all programs that have been conducted on campuses but have then been publicly exposed as inappropriate and coercive. Similar programs should also rightly be subject to challenge.

If a program seems coercive, encourage your child to raise questions and concerns. Take note of a new Foundation for Individual Rights in Education program called the Stand Up For Speech Litigation Project. This program empowers students to challenge unlawful campus speech restrictions; it also highlights students who have pushed back with dramatic success when they saw their individual liberty under threat and their rights to free speech trampled.[7] With information and expertise, third parties can also offer an independent perspective on whether the matter is coercive and inappropriate.

Sensitivity Pledges

In recent years, more and more campuses have been pushing sensitivity pledges, and these too warrant a skeptical eye. Especially prevalent are those that demand adherence to sustainability, social justice, and other matters.[8]

While many of these pledges are no doubt well-intended, the fact is that poorly conceptualized or badly executed programs can stifle thought, questions, and discussion.

Take for example Harvard's short-lived 2011 kindness pledge. A pledge to make Harvard a place "where the exercise of kindness holds a place on a par with intellectual attainment" was posted in the entryways for undergraduates. The pledge was shown together with a list of the names of the residents of the entryway together with a column of spaces for signatures, for all to see.[9]

Thanks to the protest from a former dean, and a call by others to end the "indoctrination," the pledge was publicly opposed, and was eventually shut down.[10] The fact is that this kind of feel-good initiative can seriously intrude on free speech and the robust exchange of ideas. Lesson: Urge your child to find someone on the outside to help expose programs and pledges that crowd out free thinking.

BIAS IN THE CLASSROOM

And what about bias in the classroom? As we learned earlier, there is ample evidence of imbalance in course reading lists, professors who engage in partisan political discussion, unrelated to the topic at hand, and those who convince students, rightly or wrongly, that they must agree to get a good grade. If students encounter such situations, what should they do? Should they simply suffer in silence, understanding that life is filled with challenges? Or should they take action?

For starters, have your child check in with you. It is important to remember: There is a difference between a professor who properly challenges beliefs in the pursuit of truth and one who is ignoring professional standards. A rich liberal education, after all, is about confronting difficult issues, assessing both sides of sometimes long-held and unquestioned beliefs, and learning to think for oneself. The most able professors are often those who "shake up" a student's worldview and force a healthy reevaluation.

But there is a wide gulf between appropriate academic challenge and intimidation and unprofessional behavior. If your child thinks he or she is witnessing the latter, see if others agree: have him or her compare notes with other students in the same class; or bring a friend to class to offer an independent assessment. As outlined earlier, in many cases, students have used their cell phones to tape or photograph what they believe is inappropriate behavior—a tool that can work, but that also raises real legal concerns. Some schools have grievance procedures for students who want to bring complaints about faculty professional responsibility. And organizations like Foundation for Individual Rights in Education and American Council of Trustees and Alumni can also offer advice and counsel—or point students to faculty friends who might be able to be a sounding board.

In the academy, as in life, some will be more responsible than others. That's why it's so important—early in the college selection process and then once enrolled—to look long and hard at course listings, faculty profiles, and academic requirements. More than anything else, these can offer insight on whether the school—and its faculty—are truly focused on rigorous education or more interested in pushing their own ideologies.

ANALYZING A MAJOR IN THE LIBERAL ARTS

Stories are rampant of French literature majors who cannot find a job and English concentrators who are flipping burgers rather than turning an artful phrase. Students, often with parental pushes, have been migrating away from the humanities, from English language or literature or philosophy and the like, to fields that seem to promise easier paths to employment, like the natural sciences.[11] And some governors and schools are taking a narrow and rigidly vocational view of higher education—one that steers students toward high-demand majors and preprofessional programs at the expense of a wider liberal arts background.[12]

But there is nothing wrong with the liberal arts.

The battle between advocates of the liberal arts and those who call for a narrower, ostensibly more pragmatic training for professional careers has raged for centuries.

Famed theologian and educator John Henry Cardinal Newman argued passionately in his 1852 book *The Idea of a University* that the liberal arts remain the core mission of higher education. An individual, Newman warned, "trained to think upon one subject or for one subject only, will never be a good judge even in that one: whereas the enlargement of his circle gives him increased knowledge and power in a rapidly increasing ratio."[13]

And Newman admonished his readers to remember that a liberal education is preparation not only for all careers but also for living in and serving a
community—it is to "prepare for the world."[14]

Studies show that liberal arts graduates can have considerable career success, even compared to those in more technical fields. In 1956, Bell Laboratories began scientifically tracking the career progress of staff from different
backgrounds of academic preparation. Over a twenty-year period with the
company, staff who had been liberal arts majors progressed more rapidly and
in greater percentages than their nonliberal arts counterparts.

Bell's report, released in 1981, concluded that "There is no reason for
liberal arts majors to lack confidence in approaching business careers. These
humanities and social science majors in particular continue to make a strong
showing in managerial skills and have experienced considerable business
success. We hope and expect this to continue."[15]

In a recent survey, 93 percent of employers asserted that "a candidate's
demonstrated capacity to think critically, communicate clearly, and solve
complex problems"—skills traditionally associated with the liberal arts—was
more important than the undergraduate major.[16] A majority of employers
surveyed by the Conference Board list writing, reading, comprehension, and
mathematics as very important basic skills for job success.[17] Significant numbers list science, foreign languages, and government as desirable basic skills
and necessary knowledge.

And sociologists Richard Arum and Josipa Roksa's book, *Academically
Adrift*, mentioned in chapter 1, found that students majoring in fields such as
communications and business, which so many parents promote as leading to
a good job, in fact showed some of the lowest levels of learning gain of any
fields surveyed. Liberal arts-oriented majors, by contrast, likely benefitted
from their "more-demanding reading and writing assignments."[18] Students
who "exhibited higher academic engagement/growth in college" were also
more likely to be financially secure and civically engaged after graduation.[19]

According to the Bureau of Labor Statistics, persons born between 1957
and 1964 on average held more than eleven different jobs between the ages
of eighteen and forty-eight alone.[20] A significant number of students will
find their careers taking them in directions they had not planned. Given the
dynamism of the modern marketplace, broad skills and knowledge provide
the agility graduates need, more so than locking into a narrow professional
career path early. It's frankly impossible to know what jobs will be open
when students graduate and even more difficult to know what jobs will be
available in two or three decades.

And there is ample evidence that the very majors that seem most likely during college to lead to a good job can actually hurt students, big time. Take just

the last decade. In 2003, "nearly 10 percent of students took a job in consulting. About 16 percent went into education. In 2007 the share of consultants fell to half the 2003 level; educators fell too. Finance jobs were the big gains. By 2011, finance had retreated, and education fell again, but consultants were making a modest comeback."[21]

There is absolutely nothing wrong with the liberal arts. But there are problems with many of our liberal arts colleges. The answer is not to avoid the liberal arts but to undertake majors and course selection with care (as discussed elsewhere in this book) and to understand that studying the liberal arts and getting a good job—as we have seen at colleges like Randolph-Macon—need not be mutually exclusive.

DEALING WITH FERPA AND HIPAA

In years past, parents could expect to receive timely information from the school to see how students were learning and faring. But that's harder than it used to be.

Students are deemed adults under the deceptively named FERPA (Family Educational Rights and Privacy Act), which, for all intents and purposes, provides no rights to parents for private information—even when they are paying—once their child turns eighteen or enters a postsecondary institution. Schools may—but are not required to—share information about an eligible student's records with parents, without the student's consent when:

- Parents claim the student as a dependent for tax purposes.
- If a health or safety emergency involves their son or daughter.
- If the student is under twenty-one and has violated any law or policy concerning alcohol or controlled substances.
- Information is based on a school official's personal knowledge and observation of the student.[22]

What's a parent to do?

If possible, work this out with your child in advance. Make it clear that you expect to see his or her report cards. And if that's not enough, work with your child to craft a written release to the academic institution waiving privacy and instructing the school to provide grades to you. This means that you will be able to see how your child is doing in the classroom.

And stay involved when it comes to your child's mental, emotional, and physical health as well. A recent study at Penn State University showed that parent-based intervention, especially before college, as simple as discussion of the dangers of alcohol abuse, can be highly effective in curbing heavy drinking patterns.[23]

More than a few college students experience medical problems of some kind during their college stay, including emotional or mental health issues. Parents wanting to know about these matters face yet another layer of difficulty in getting information—over and above FERPA restrictions. Privacy restrictions under the Health Insurance Portability and Accountability Act (HIPAA) prohibit parents in most cases from talking to medical personnel at the school or local medical facility without the child's permission.

Your involvement in your child's health matters ultimately depends on your relationship.

If you want to learn about your child's health or believe there may be a need to act in the future because of your child's chronic medical condition, you should ask him or her in advance to sign a HIPAA authorization—a permission slip granting you the right to talk to particular doctors as well as a medical power of attorney that will allow you to make medical decisions as your child's legal agent. In the absence of such documents, neither college nor medical personnel are generally authorized to talk to you. For additional guidance, you may want to take a look at a very helpful article in *Consumer Reports*, which is included in the endnotes.[24]

When parents don't have that access, the stories can be tragic. Take the case of one young man enrolled in a prestigious liberal arts college in the Northeast. The student had been a top student, but in the second semester of his senior year, took quite a turn for the worse. His grades had plummeted, and his mental health, too—with evidence of substantial alcohol and substance abuse.

Because of the various legal restrictions, the parents learned about their child's sad decline after it was too late. The boy dropped out and had to be placed in rehabilitation and therapy. Ultimately, he returned to school and finished, but only after the parents found themselves faced with unexpected medical bills and an additional semester of tuition.

SUMMING UP

Helping your child select the right college is only the start of the story. As outlined in this chapter, staying involved—during the college years—is just as important. The college experience entails a range of decisions—picking a course schedule, selecting a major, and making healthy choices—that can benefit from continuing and sensitive parental engagement.

Chapter 12

Conclusion: Jump Right In!

So, there you have it! Armed with this guidebook, you are now ready to go. Selecting a college may be stressful, but you should also make sure it is fun.

There are thousands of four-year residential institutions around the country—known and unknown, beautiful and not so. They have many differences when it comes to quality and cost. But *all* of them are joyous testimonies to Americans' love of learning—to the belief and recognition that our democratic republic deserves an educated citizenry.

Liberty and learning go together.

Washington and the Founders understood that ignorance and freedom cannot coexist. A shared understanding and a shared knowledge help unify and advance civilization. "If a nation expects to be ignorant and free," Thomas Jefferson wrote, "in a state of civilization, it expects what never was and never will be."[1]

Jefferson wrote the Declaration of Independence, but he was also a trustee and founder of the University of Virginia, which remains "Mr. Jefferson's University"; Madison was the father of the Constitution, but he was also a trustee of Hampden-Sydney.[2] Hamilton was a trustee of Columbia.[3] Franklin helped to found the University of Pennsylvania.[4] George Washington helped make Washington and Lee what it is today.[5] The list goes on and on.

And this wasn't serendipity. It was because our great Founding Fathers understood better than anyone that an excellent college education should and would help undergird a nation founded on a set of abstract propositions dedicated to "life, liberty, and the pursuit of happiness."

They understood that the strength of our society is directly dependent on the strength of the education our schools provide.

So, one more time: What's a parent to do?

With your informed participation, you can help ensure that our colleges and universities advance academic excellence, academic freedom, and accountability.

You can embrace the challenge of helping find a great college for your child.

And with thoughtfulness, energy, and cheer, you can mark this turning point in the life of your family by asking good questions, getting answers, and making your decision together.

Postscript: Take Action

Well, parents, it's been a pleasure traveling this road together. And now that the selection process is over—or nearly done—consider going one step further.

As you've learned, higher education remains a remarkably opaque industry. Given its size and importance, it is frankly mindboggling how hard it is to figure out how colleges and universities are doing and what you are getting for your money.

So, consider taking action. Here are just a few ideas for your consideration:

HELP PUT AN END TO SPEECH CODES

If your child is looking at a public institution with a *red light* speech code—or is actually attending one—write to the board of trustees and demand that the speech code be ended. You can call the American Council of Trustees and Alumni for help to obtain the names and addresses of trustees for your letter. Two, send the letter to your state legislators and demand that they get involved. Ask them to ask the college why it is violating the First Amendment and urge them to condition future funding on the school's pledge that it will abide by the Constitution.

Urge your legislators to adopt model legislation that would end unconstitutional free speech zones at public schools in the state. The proposed bill in Appendix B was drafted by the Foundation on Individual Rights in Education and modeled after House Bill 258, signed by the Virginia governor, prohibiting public colleges "from imposing restrictions on time, place, and manner of student speech that occurs in the outdoor areas of the institution's campus."[1]

SHED LIGHT ON COURSE OFFERINGS

While it's far preferable for institutions themselves to provide course listings and readings for students and the public to see, if they don't, encourage your state legislature to insist on it. Texas has already adopted a syllabus bill—and more states should do the same. A sample bill is located in Appendix B. Alternatively, ask the institution to mandate that faculty outline courses and course readings by a certain deadline. At the University of Virginia, for example, students receive thousands of course titles but little meaningful information on which to make their course decisions.

INSIST ON EVIDENCE OF STUDENT LEARNING

There are a few systems of voluntary accountability, but—all in all—many schools refuse to participate or publicize their findings. It's pretty hard to believe, given the trillions of dollars we are spending on higher education—but the fact is that parents and policymakers are too often left in the dark then it comes to understanding what students are learning. As a parent, you can help change this. Ask the schools whether they have any assessments of student learning gains, and ask where you can find them.

Go to your legislator and insist that he or she adopt a bill that will require taxpayer-funded institutions to use valid, nationally normed assessments of what students are learning and demand transparency. You can find a draft bill to take to your legislator in Appendix B and ACTA will be happy to help.

HELP RESTORE THE FIVE-DAY WEEK

There is troubling evidence that the pathologies we see on our college campus—sexual assault, drinking, and substance abuse—are a by-product of a culture that puts less and less emphasis on rigorous academic work. One of the ways to address this problem is to insist that students and faculty actually study and learn from Monday to Friday, not just Tuesday to Thursday as is so often the case now. In Appendix B, you will find a model bill that will require leaders of colleges and universities to examine how they use their buildings, before they build any more. There is more than one way to skin a cat.

Acknowledgments

This book would not have been possible without the founders, staff, and supporters of the American Council of Trustees and Alumni (ACTA).

For the past twenty years, I have had the good fortune to work alongside some of the best policy wonks, recent college graduates, and passionate trustees anyone could ask for. The information in this book is, in so many ways, the work of all of them.

Thinking back to the early days of ACTA's existence, special thanks are due to several individuals: first, to the founding president Dr. Jerry L. Martin. There are few individuals of Jerry's equal. A great writer, a prodigious thinker, a tremendous mentor and friend, Jerry is the kind of professor we all hoped to find—fully informed, articulate, caring, and insistent on high standards. And unlike most in the professoriate, he is proof that an academic can also be an entrepreneur, and an astute political strategist as well.

Thanks are similarly due to Dr. Stephen Balch, now head of the Institute for the Study of Western Civilization at Texas Tech University, and at the time of ACTA's founding, president of the National Association of Scholars (NAS). Steve had founded NAS in order to give a voice to faculty who believed that higher education must be committed to merit, not political fashion, and that understanding the heritage of our country and the duties of citizenship are essential goals of a college education. He felt there was also a need for trustees and alumni to weigh in and helped engender the ideas that ultimately became ACTA.

Both Steve and Jerry were eminent academics, published authors, and engaged instructors. Thanks to their love of the academy, these two were able to see—as did other ACTA founders—that the quality of American higher education was threatened, not by a lack of funding, or by intrusive trustees and legislators, but by often politically correct forces on the *inside of the academy*—who were, too often, putting their own interests ahead of the interests of students and the public, without any countervailing force.

Over many years in difficult circumstances and with considerable courage, they and others were willing to withstand the personal attacks and opprobrium levied upon them by academic insiders who were loath to let the sunlight in—thank you, Justice Holmes!—that ACTA demanded shine on the billion dollar operation known as American higher education.

But, of course, every good idea also needs to be sustained. And in that category, there are so many wonderful "sustainers"—I know I cannot adequately credit them all. Indeed, Armand Alacbay, Hank Brown, Roxie Burris, Sandra E. Diaz, Thor Halvorssen, Lauri Kempson, Barry Latzer, Rich Lizardo, Jacquie Merrill, Judy Miles, Charles Mitchell, Rick O'Donnell, Michael Poliakoff, and Alexis Zhang are just a few of the terrific individuals who have—over the past twenty years—helped make ACTA the force to be reckoned with when it comes to higher education reform.

Many of these same people deserve credit for providing great content and feedback on chapters and the entire manuscript. Special thanks to Dr. Richard Vedder of Ohio University who agreed to author chapter 9: *Learn the Real Cost*. Richard is a good friend, an economic historian, and an expert on college finance who I knew would help ensure a handy guide to paying for college.

Joining them are other friends and colleagues including Dr. Karl Borden, Dr. Stuart Butler and Jamie Butler, Carmen Diaz, William Gonch, and Dr. Philip Bretton, who proved most talented in his ability to track down the sources, numbers, and details that are the necessary underpinnings of any higher education story.

Deserving recognition—too—are the many generous and inspirational supporters of ACTA who suggested a book along these lines. From the beginning, these were the individuals and foundations who believed that the mission of higher education was teaching, learning, and the pursuit of truth; who believed that students should be given a strong liberal education that enables them to live thoughtful lives, informed by the study of the highest achievements of human civilization; and who understood that rational debate and the free exchange of ideas are essential to higher ed's mission and that affordable tuitions are critical to the American dream.

They realized what remains true today—academic freedom and high academic standards are important to everyone in a democracy.

To them all, I extend most hearty and heartfelt thanks.

Selecting a College Checklist

CHECKLIST

Here is a checklist of important topics and information you'll want to investigate for each of the schools you are exploring.

THE SCHOOL

- Does the school give students a strong foundation of skills and knowledge? (go to www.whatwilltheylearn.com)
- What percentage of students are in-state and out-of-state? (check out school website)
- Male/female ratios (school website)
- Admission deadlines and percentage admitted (school website)
- Pass rates on licensure exams (school website)
- Catalog/syllabi/course information? (school website)
- Faculty profiles (school website)
- Does the school have an oasis of excellence? (check out oases of excellence, www.goacta.org)

Name of oasis: _____

- Is there a career services office with placement initiatives and counseling?

COST/FINANCIAL HEALTH

Can we afford this school? Check out:

- College Reality Check, Chronicle of Higher Education https://collegereality check.com/en/
- Big future, www.bigfuture.collegeboard.org
- Net Price Calculator, http://netpricecalculator.collegeboard.org/
- College Scorecard, https://collegescorecard.ed.gov/
- Is the school financially sound? (see Moody's Higher Education Ratings https://www.moodys.com/credit-ratings/)
- What percentage of the class graduates in four years? (see www.whatwill theylearn.com and www.collegeresults.org)
- Do students get good jobs after graduating? (visit www.payscale.com)

FREE SPEECH

- Is the school committed to free speech? (check www.thefire.org; www. whatwilltheylearn.com; and www.heterodoxacademy.org)
- Is there a student code of conduct? (go to the school website and enter "Student Code of Conduct")
- Have there been any recent speaker disinvitations? (Google the name of the school and "disinvitation" to see if the school is hostile to diverse speakers)

CAMPUS CULTURE

- What kind of residential arrangements does the school have? (see school website)
- Is it a party school? (consult Princeton Review http://www.princetonreview. com/college-rankings?rankings=party-schools; https://colleges.niche.com/ rankings/top-party-schools/
- How much crime is there on campus? (see Clery Act data, http://ope.ed.gov/ security/)
- Are students engaged? (search for "NSSE" on the school website)
- Does the school show whether its students are learning? (check out Voluntary System of Accountability, www.collegeportraits.org)
- What do students think of professors there? (see Rate my professor www. ratemyprofessor.com)

Appendix A

Share This Letter.
Advice to College Freshmen

By Greg Lewin[1]

Dear Future College Students:

Congratulations! You've been accepted into college! If I may, I'd like to share some of my ideas on what it means to go to college, and how to select a college and college program that will prepare you for all of the important things you want to accomplish.

Looking back, it's amazing to examine how much changes between the ages of eighteen and twenty-two. According to law, when we turn eighteen, a switch is flipped and we become adults. Suddenly we can vote, we can choose where we live, we can decide what classes we take in college.

Choosing which courses to take in college may not seem like a huge decision. Checking boxes to fulfill a patchwork of requirements seems almost too easy. But in essence, you are asking yourself, "What knowledge will equip me with the wisdom required to make life's big decisions?"

At least, that's what you should be asking yourself. That particular question was never posed by Freshman Greg. Instead, Freshman Greg set to tackling such imponderables as, "Will this class fit in my schedule?" "Will this professor be fun?" and "Does putting hot dogs in my oatmeal count as breakfast or dinner?"

At eighteen, I did not identify the gaps in my fundamental knowledge. I did not choose classes that would help fill these gaps and prepare me for the real world. Though legally I was an adult, truthfully I was a college kid who didn't know any better. And no one told me otherwise.

In fact, colleges across the country have loosened curricular requirements to attract more students. It's the same reason why so many schools are building state-of-the-art facilities (and passing the bill onto the students in the form of increased tuition prices). Today, according to the *What Will They Learn?* study, only 35 percent of colleges require a college-level literature course.

Just 18 percent require an American history or government course, and a paltry 3 percent require economics.

It worries me that in times like these, so many students are graduating without fundamental courses that I—and quite a number of employers—believe are important for life beyond college. Of the over 1,100 schools evaluated, only twenty-five earned an "A" rating in What Will They Learn? for the strength of their curriculum. Some are small private schools enrolling a few hundred kids, but a school need not be tiny to be selective about its academic program. The past president of the University of Georgia, an "A" school which boasts an undergraduate population of over 26,000 students, made a statement about this evaluation. I think his words perfectly sum up the vision that informs a well-designed academic program: "In an era of cafeteria course loads at many places, where students are free to choose from an array of courses, this place has remained steadfast in the belief that in the first two years, all students should have a similar liberal arts foundation laid in preparation for the specialization to come."

It is true that you can get a great education from almost any school in the country. The bad news is that the quality of the education is, in many cases, up to you, and many schools will provide little guidance. If you want a solid foundational education you don't have to go to one of the twenty-five colleges that earn an "A" rating. You can build your own education—and What Will They Learn? can serve as a guide for the type of education that employers want, our country needs, and will serve you long after graduation. But at many colleges and universities, the burden will be on you to make these informed choices.

John Engler, former governor of Michigan and president of the Business Roundtable, has noted with alarm the shortcomings in college curricula: "Too few schools require their students to develop a firm grounding in core subject areas, the foundation upon which later expertise can be built. This does a disservice not only to the students but also to employers seeking the capable, well-rounded employees they need to compete in the global economy." In other words, there are consequences in the job market for poor choices in college.

The fact is, even if some students are well-prepared for college, many will not have studied literature, science, math, economics, and the other fields of knowledge essential for success at a truly collegiate level.

Knowing what I now know, I wonder why the adults often "dumb down" existing requirements and ignore the existing gaps that allow students to graduate without the skills and knowledge that will help them succeed after graduation.

If I could go back and give some advice to Freshman Greg, it would be to not only take courses that pique my interest or fit conveniently into my schedule but also to take a wide array of foundational courses that would help me in the future.

Model Legislation

CAMPUS FREE EXPRESSION ACT

To amend chapter ___, by adding thereto one new section relating to free speech at public institutions of higher education.

Be it enacted by the General Assembly of the State, as follows:

Section 1. Chapter___, is amended by adding thereto one new section, to be known as section___, to read as follows:

(a) Expressive activities protected under the provisions of this section include, but are not limited to, all forms of peaceful assembly, protests, speeches, distribution of literature, carrying signs, and circulating petitions.

(b) The outdoor areas of campuses of public institutions of higher education in this state shall be deemed traditional public forums. Public institutions of higher education may maintain and enforce reasonable time, place, and manner restrictions in service of a significant institutional interest only when such restrictions employ clear, published, content, and viewpoint-neutral criteria, and provide for ample alternative means of expression. Any such restrictions shall allow for members of the university community to spontaneously and contemporaneously assemble and distribute literature.

(c) Any person who wishes to engage in noncommercial expressive activity on campus shall be permitted to do so freely, as long as the person's conduct is not unlawful and does not materially and substantially disrupt the functioning of the institution subject to the requirements of subsection 2 of this section.

(d) Nothing in this section shall be interpreted as limiting the right of student expression elsewhere on campus.

(e) The following persons may bring an action in a court of competent jurisdiction to enjoin any violation of this section or to recover compensatory
damages, reasonable court costs, and attorney fees:

    (1) The attorney general;
    (2) Persons whose expressive rights were violated through the violation
        of this section.

(f) In an action brought under subsection 5 of this section, if the court finds
a violation, the court shall award the aggrieved persons no less than
$500 for the initial violation, plus $50 for each day the violation remains
ongoing.

(g) A person shall be required to bring suit for violation of this section not
later than one year after the day the cause of action accrues. For purposes
of calculating the one-year limitation period, each day that the violation
persists, and each day that a policy in violation of this section remains
in effect, shall constitute a new violation of this section and, therefore, a
new day that the cause of action has accrued.

TRANSPARENCY IN COURSE OFFERINGS ACT

Be it enacted by the [STATE] legislature:

Section 1

(a) Each publicly funded institution of higher education shall make available
to the public on the institution's Internet website the following information for each undergraduate course offered for credit by the institution:

    (1) A syllabus that

        i. Satisfies any standards adopted by the institution;
        ii. Provides a brief description of each major course requirement,
            including each major assignment and examination;
        iii. Lists any required or recommended reading; and
        iv. Provides a general description of the subject matter of each lec-
            ture or discussion;

    (2) A curriculum vitae of each regular instructor that lists the instructor's

        i. Postsecondary education;
        ii. Teaching experience;
        iii. Significant professional publications; and

(3) If available, a departmental budget report of the department under which the course is offered, from the most recent semester or other academic term during which the institution offered the course.

(b) A curriculum vitae made available on the institution's Internet website under Subsection (a) may not include any personal information, including the instructor's home address or home telephone number.

(c) The information required by Subsection (a) must be

(1) Accessible from the institution's Internet website home page by use of not more than three links;
(2) Searchable by keywords and phrases; and
(3) Accessible to the public without requiring registration or use of a username, a password, or another user identification.

(d) The institution shall make the information required by Subsection (a) available not later than the seventh day after the first day of classes for the semester or other academic term during which the course is offered. The institution shall continue to make the information available on the institution's Internet website until at least the second anniversary of the date on which the institution initially posted the information.

(e) The institution shall update the information required by Subsection (a) as soon as practicable after the information changes.

(f) The governing body of the institution shall designate an administrator to be responsible for ensuring implementation of this section. The administrator may assign duties under this section to one or more administrative employees.

(g) Not later than January 1 of each odd-numbered year, each institution of higher education shall submit a written report regarding the institution's compliance with this section to the governor, the lieutenant governor, the speaker of the house of representatives, and the presiding officer of each legislative standing committee with primary jurisdiction over higher education.

(h) The [STATE] [Higher Education Coordination Board/Department of Education] may adopt rules necessary to administer this section.

ASSESSING COLLEGIATE SKILLS ACT

Be it enacted by the [STATE] legislature:

Section 1. The following provisions shall apply to all institutions of public higher education that award baccalaureate degrees.

(a) Each institution shall annually assess the level of student learning gains in core collegiate skills, which include, at a minimum, writing and analytical reasoning/critical thinking.

(b) Institutions will assess core collegiate skills using a standardized, nationally normed instrument, such as the Collegiate Learning Assessment, administered by the Council on Aid to Education; the Collegiate Assessment of Academic Proficiency, administered by ACT, Inc.; or the Proficiency Profile, administered by Educational Testing Services, Inc.

(c) Beginning [DATE], each institution shall report the following results for student learning gains in core collegiate skills annually on its website:

   (1) Average freshman score on a nationally normed assessment instrument testing core collegiate skills;
   (2) Average rising junior or senior score on the same assessment instrument for core collegiate skills used to test the freshman cohort; and
   (3) Comparison of the student learning gains in core collegiate skills with the predicted learning gains of students with similar academic profiles.

Section 2. The [STATE] [Higher Education Coordination Board/Department of Education] shall adopt rules to administer Section 1 of this Act. Such rules shall include options for institutions to choose between longitudinal assessment and randomly selected cohorts of students, a requirement for value-added assessment of writing skills and analytical reasoning/critical thinking, and minimum cohort size.

KNOW BEFORE YOU BUILD ACT

Be it enacted by the [STATE] legislature:

Section 1

(a) Each institution of public higher education shall develop and make publicly available procedures for full utilization of existing facilities, including plans for the use of distance and online education.

(b) Each institution of public higher education shall post on its website each year data on the utilization of classroom and laboratory facilities. Such data will include:

   (1) Total number of classrooms and laboratories available for instructional use, separately reporting those undergoing renovation;
   (2) Total available square footage of instructional space, separately reporting that under renovation;
   (3) Average weekly hours of instructional usage of all campus classrooms and laboratories available for instruction, reported by day of the week and time of day, Monday through Saturday inclusive;

(4) Average percentage of seats/stations filled in all sections taught in campus classrooms and laboratories that are available for instruction, reported by day of the week and time of day, Monday through Saturday inclusive; and

(5) The number of courses the institution currently offers online, and plans for future development of online courses.

(c) Beginning [DATE], each institution of higher education shall submit a written report summarizing the data set forth above to the governor, the lieutenant governor, the speaker of the house of representatives, and the presiding officer of each legislative standing committee with jurisdiction over higher education.

Section 2

(a) When determining whether to approve the capital budget of any proposed new building or facility, the governing board of a public university shall hold public discussion. Such discussion shall proceed whether funding comes from public or private sources. Discussion will include, but not be limited to:

(1) Level of utilization of existing campus buildings, using the metrics described in Section 1 earlier, for the preceding three-year period;

(2) Projected maintenance costs for the proposed building over its projected lifetime; and

(3) Funding sources for the proposed building.

(b) This section shall not apply to proposed projects that do not exceed $10,000,000 in total cost.

Notes

PREFACE

1. Grace Kena et al., *The Condition of Education 2015*, NCES 2015–144 (Washington, DC: National Center for Education Statistics, 2015), 184, Indicator 30, http://nces.ed.gov/pubs2015/2015144.pdf.

2. Mark Sklarow, "Trends in Independent Educational Consulting 2016" (presentation, Independent Educational Consultants Association Webinar, n.p., December 8, 2015), https://www.iecaonline.com/PDF/IECA_State-of-Profession-2016.pdf. The Independent Educational Consultants Association estimates that the total number of independent admissions consultants leapt from 4–5,000 in 2005 to 17–23,000 in 2015. The National Association for College Admissions Counselors is a 15,000-member organization for admissions and counseling professionals. For more, see http://www.nacacnet.org/Pages/default.aspx.

3. *Boosting Postsecondary Education Performance: A Statement by the Policy and Impact Committee for Economic Development* (Washington, DC: Committee on Economic Development, 2012), 9, https://www.ced.org/reports/single/boosting-postsecondary-education-performance.

4. Emily Dai, "Student Loan Delinquencies Surge," *Inside the Vault*, Federal Reserve Bank of St. Louis, Spring 2013, https://www.stlouisfed.org/Publications/Inside-The-Vault/Spring-2013/Student-Loan-Delinquencies-Surge. For more on the grim real-life stories of college grads moving home, see Adam Davidson, "It's Official: The Boomerang Kids Won't Leave," *New York Times Magazine*, June 20, 2014, http://www.nytimes.com/2014/06/22/magazine/its-official-the-boomerang-kids-wont-leave.html?_r=0#.

5. *Education at a Glance 2014: OECD Indicators* (Paris: OECD, 2014), 207, Chart B1.2a, http://www.oecd.org/edu/Education-at-a-Glance-2014.pdf.

6. Victor Luckerson, "The Myth of the Four-Year College Degree," *TIME*, January 10, 2013, http://business.time.com/2013/01/10/the-myth-of-the-4-year-college-degree/.

7. Several studies demonstrate the limited studying that college students undertake. See "American Time Use Survey," *Bureau of Labor Statistics*, last modified October 26, 2015, http://www.bls.gov/tus/charts/students.htm; "NSSE 2014 U.S. Grand Frequencies By Carnegie Classification," *National Survey of Student Engagement*, 13, question 15, http://nsse.indiana.edu/2014_institutional_report/pdf/Frequencies/Freq%20-%20SR%20by%20Carn.pdf; and Jennifer Epstein, "Anything But Studying," *Inside Higher Ed*, February 9, 2010, https://www.insidehighered.com/news/2010/02/09/california. About 70 percent of respondents expressed the belief that a core curriculum ought to be part of a college education in a 2011 Roper survey commissioned by the American Council of Trustees and Alumni. See "Memo RE: ACTA Survey Findings," *American Council of Trustees and Alumni with GfK Roper Public Affairs & Media*, August 2011, http://whatwilltheylearn.com/public/pdfs/RoperFindings.pdf. Discontent with outcomes is rife among graduates, according to a report by McKinsey & Company. About 53 percent of respondents "would do something differently," by choosing a different college, a different major, or both. André Dua, *Voice of the Graduate* (New York, NY: McKinsey & Company in collaboration with Chegg, Inc., 2013), 11–12, http://mckinseyonsociety.com/downloads/reports/Education/UXC001%20Voice%20of%20the%20Graduate%20v7.pdf.

8. "The Rising Cost of Not Going to College," *Pew Research Center*, February 11, 2014, http://www.pewsocialtrends.org/2014/02/11/the-rising-cost-of-not-going-to-college/.

9. *Digest of Education Statistics, 2014* (Washington, DC: National Center for Education Statistics, n.d.), Table 317.10, https://nces.ed.gov/programs/digest/d14/tables/dt14_317.10.asp?current=yes. Included on this table are data for "4-year public" and "4-year nonprofit private" institutions.

10. *The 2013 Lumina Study of the American Public's Opinion on Higher Education and U.S. Business Leaders Poll on Higher Education: What America Needs to Know about Higher Education Redesign* (Indianapolis, IN: Gallup, Inc. and Lumina Foundation, 2014), 29, http://www.gallup.com/services/176759/america-needs-know-higher-education-redesign.aspx.

CHAPTER 1

1. Sandy Baum and Jennifer Ma, *Trends in College Pricing 2014* in *Trends in Higher Education* series (n.p.: College Board, 2014), 17, Table 2a, http://trends.collegeboard.org/sites/default/files/2014-trends-college-pricing-final-web.pdf.

2. "Digest of Education Statistics: Table 303.40," *National Center for Education Statistics*, 2013, http://nces.ed.gov/programs/digest/d13/tables/dt13_303.40.asp.

3. The National Association of Independent Colleges and Universities includes on its website mention of nontraditional students: "Private colleges are expanding flexible learning models, online courses, hybrid programs, three-year degree programs, and satellite campuses. They offer degree and certificate programs developed for adult learners, with many classes offered at night, on the weekends, partially or fully online, and during the summer. A large number of private colleges have transfer

agreements with community colleges." See "9 Myths about Private Nonprofit Higher Education," *National Association of Independent Colleges and Universities*, http://www.naicu.edu/special_initiatives/nine_myths/. In 2006, education journalist Kate Zernike reported that 60 percent of college students attend more than one school, in "College, My Way," *New York Times*, April 23, 2006, http://www.nytimes.com/2006/04/23/education/edlife/zernike.html?pagewanted=all.

4. "Tuition and Fees and Room and Board over Time, 1975–76 to 2015–16, Selected Years," Trends in College Pricing, *College Board*, n.d., http://trends.college board.org/college-pricing/figures-tables/tuition-and-fees-and-room-and-board-over-time-1975-76-2015-16-selected-years.

5. Federal Reserve Bank of New York, "Household Debt Continues Upward Climb while Student Loan Delinquencies Worsen," press release, February 17, 2015, https://www.newyorkfed.org/newsevents/news/research/2015/rp150217.html.

6. "Even at state flagship universities—selective, research-intensive institutions—only 36 percent of full-time students complete their bachelor's degree on time," writes Tamar Lewin in "Most College Students Don't Earn a Degree in 4 Years, Study Finds," *New York Times*, December 1, 2014, http://www.nytimes.com/2014/12/02/education/most-college-students-dont-earn-degree-in-4-years-study-finds.html?_r=0. For more, see *Four-Year Myth* (Indianapolis, IN: Complete College America, 2014), http://completecollege.org/wp-content/uploads/2014/11/4-Year-Myth.pdf.

7. Preety Sidhu and Valerie J. Calderon, "Many Business Leaders Doubt U.S. Colleges Prepare Students," *Gallup*, February 26, 2014, http://www.gallup.com/poll/167630/business-leaders-doubt-colleges-prepare-students.aspx.

8. Scott Jaschik, "'Academically Adrift,'" *Inside Higher Ed*, January 18, 2011, https://www.insidehighered.com/news/2011/01/18/study_finds_large_numbers_of_college_students_don_t_learn_much.

9. Janna Herron, "Survey: Student Loan Debt Forces Many to Put Life on Hold," *Bankrate*, August 5, 2015, http://www.bankrate.com/finance/consumer-index/money-pulse-0815.aspx.

10. Nick Anderson and Danielle Douglas-Gabriel, "Nation's Prominent Public Universities Are Shifting to Out-of-State Students," *Washington Post*, January 30, 2016, https://www.washingtonpost.com/local/education/nations-prominent-public-universities-are-shifting-to-out-of-state-students/2016/01/30/07575790-beaf-11e5-bcda-62a36b 394160_story.html.

11. Jon Marcus, "Student Subsidies of Classmates' Tuition Add to Anger over Rising College Costs," *Hechinger Report*, August 29, 2012, http://hechingerreport.org/student-subsidies-of-classmates-tuition-add-to-anger-over-rising-college-costs/.

12. Danielle Douglas-Gabriel, "Middle-Class Families Are Fed Up with Their Financial Aid Options," *Washington Post*, January 29, 2015, http://www.washington post.com/news/get-there/wp/2015/01/29/middle-class-families-are-fed-up-with-their-financial-aid-options/. Douglas-Gabriel explains, "Federal dollars are divvied up in a way that tends to shut out families making more than $50,000 and less than $100,000. Pell grants generally wind up in the hands of students whose families earn

less than the median household income of $53,000. On the other hand, education tax credits mostly go to families making at least $100,000."

13. Jeffrey J. Selingo, *College (Un)bound: The Future of Higher Education and What It Means for Students* (New York, NY: Houghton Mifflin Harcourt, 2013), 59. Parents can learn basic methods of evaluating the fiscal condition of colleges from the following two articles in *Forbes*. Grades for fiscal health are issued to 900 private four-year colleges, and the grading system is explained. The system includes such principles as the acknowledgment that heavy reliance on tuition as a source of revenue is a sign of instability. See Matt Schifrin, "Is Your College Going Broke? The Most and Least Financially Fit Schools in America," *Forbes*, August 13, 2013, http://www.forbes.com/sites/schifrin/2013/07/24/is-your-college-going-broke/; and Matt Schifrin, "Behind Forbes College Financial Grades," *Forbes*, August 13, 2013, http://www.forbes.com/sites/schifrin/2013/07/24/behind-forbes-financial-grades/.

14. Susan Fitzgerald et al., "The Financial & Strategic Outlook for Private Colleges," (presentation, 2015 Presidents Institute, Council of Independent Colleges, San Diego, CA, January 4–7, 2015), http://www.cic.edu/News-and-Publications/Multimedia-Library/CICConferencePresentations/2015%20Presidents%20Institute/20150105-The%20Financial%20and%20Strategic%20Outlook%20for%20Private%20Colleges%205.pdf; for the Forbes information, refer to endnote 10.

CHAPTER 2

1. Karl Borden, e-mail message to author, August 6, 2013.

2. Per Google Maps, Sewanee is fifty miles from Chattanooga and from the University of Tennessee–Chattanooga. See https://www.google.com/maps.

3. The method of registering Sewanee's incoming freshmen for classes is an indication of academic seriousness. Faculty actually do this registration. In the spring before classes start, incoming freshmen take a foreign language placement exam, send in a form with descriptions of their academic experiences and interests, and are in turn registered by a faculty committee. Faculty do the work in good cheer because their role helps provide for a good experience for all. See Colleen Flaherty, "Advising Freshmen, Empowering Faculty," *Inside Higher Ed*, September 3, 2014, https://www.insidehighered.com/news/2014/09/03/sewanee-puts-faculty-back-charge-freshman-advising.

4. Rachel Fishman, *2015 College Decisions Survey: Part II: The Application Process* (Washington, DC: New America, 2015), 4, https://static.newamerica.org/attachments/3466-deciding-to-go-to-college-2/The_Application_Process.9826c29bfff54184a7a8857e6d4bb4a0.pdf. These statistics are drawn from the National Center for Education Statistics' *2012 National Postsecondary Student Aid Study*.

5. Richard Pérez-Peña, "University of California Is Set to Raise Tuition," *New York Times*, November 19, 2014, http://www.nytimes.com/2014/11/20/us/university-of-california-tuition-is-set-to-increase.html.

6. "Facts at a Glance: Fall Term 2004, Fourth Week," *University of Oregon Office of the Registrar*, n.d., https://registrar.uoregon.edu/sites/registrar2.uoregon.edu/files/

uo-facts-at-a-glance-200401-fall-2004.pdf; "Facts at a Glance: Fall Term 2015, Fourth Week," *University of Oregon Office of the Registrar*, n.d., https://registrar.uoregon. edu/sites/registrar2.uoregon.edu/files/uo-facts-at-a-glance-201501-fall-2015.pdf; and "Fall 2014 Total New Freshmen Enrollment at a Glance: The University of Alabama," *University of Alabama Office of Institutional Research & Assessment*, n.d., http://oira.ua.edu/d/sites/all/files/reports14/New_Freshman_Enrollment_at_a_ glance_All_201440.pdf.

7. "Affordability," *Harvard College Admissions & Financial Aid*, n.d., https:// college.harvard.edu/admissions/choosing-harvard/affordability; and Jordan Weissmann, "The Myth that Middle-Class Students Don't Get Financial Aid," *Slate*, January 27, 2015, http://www.slate.com/blogs/moneybox/2015/01/27/do_middle_ class_college_students_get_financial_aid_yes.html.

8. These data were exported from IPEDS, the "Integrated Postsecondary Education Data System," *National Center for Education Statistics*, n.d., http://nces. ed.gov/ipeds/. Each year, colleges and universities across the country report a wide variety of information that is stored in IPEDS to the U.S. Department of Education. The reported information can be viewed easily through College Navigator, a rich, user-friendly resource, and good place to compare schools. For more, see http://nces. ed.gov/collegenavigator/.

9. "'A' List," *What Will They Learn?*, 2016, http://whatwilltheylearn. com/a-list. Codes of conduct are often found in student handbooks. For example, see "Colorado Christian University 2016/2017," *Colorado Christian University*, 2016, http://www.ccu.edu/uploadedFiles/Pages/Campus_Life/handbook.pdf; and "Rules of Residence," *Thomas Aquinas College*, n.d., https://thomasaquinas.edu/admission/ rules-residence.

10. Scholarship America, "Get Money for College through ROTC Programs," *U.S. News & World Report*, July 25, 2013, http://www.usnews.com/education/blogs/ the-scholarship-coach/2013/07/25/get-money-for-college-through-rotc-programs; Michael Melia, "ROTC Programs Return to Ivy League Universities," *NBCNews. com*, October 23, 2011, http://www.nbcnews.com/id/45006571/ns/us_news-life/t/ rotc-programs-return-ivy-league-universities/; and Daniel Fisher, "Harvard's Love-Hate Relationship with the U.S. Military," *Defense One*, April 13, 2016, http://www. defenseone.com/ideas/2016/04/harvards-love-hate-relationship-military/127478/. But, as with any aspect of the college search, the devil is in the details. The main issues are travel to battalion exercises and availability and portability and creditworthiness of the required military science coursework. Some campuses are hosts to a battalion. Others support only crosstown membership in a battalion. And it differs from service to service. Host status tends to speak to availability of resources, but its importance varies with circumstances. Electronic college locators on ROTC armed services websites organize crosstown universities under host universities for the fifty states.

11. Penn's Naval ROTC required classes list identifies as eligible the School of Nursing, the School of Engineering and Applied Science, and the Wharton School of Business, on a listing of required classes, in "Course Requirements for All NROTC Midshipmen," *Penn NROTC*, n.d., http://www.vpul.upenn.edu/nrotc/required.html. See also "Naval Science: Spring 2017 Course & Room Roster," *University of*

Pennsylvania, Student Registration & Financial Services, last updated September 9, 2016, http://www.upenn.edu/registrar/roster/nsci.html.

12. Tapley Stephenson, "Some ROTC Courses to Receive Credit," *Yale Daily News*, November 8, 2011, http://yaledailynews.com/blog/2011/11/08/some-rotc-courses-to-receive-credit/. In the case of Air Force ROTC, only one in five courses in the academic year 2016–2017 counts toward a bachelor's degree from Yale. See the 2016–2017 Bulletin: Yale College Programs of Study, http://catalog.yale.edu/ycps/subjects-of-instruction/aerospace-studies/#coursestext.

13. Mark Hugo Lopez and Ana Gonzalez-Barrera, "Women's College Enrollment Gains Leave Men Behind," *Fact Tank: News in the Numbers* (blog), *Pew Research Center*, March 6, 2014, http://www.pewresearch.org/fact-tank/2014/03/06/womens-college-enrollment-gains-leave-men-behind/; and Jeff Guo, "Women Are Dominating Men at College. Blame Sexism," *Washington Post*, December 11, 2014, http://www.washingtonpost.com/news/storyline/wp/2014/12/11/women-are-dominating-men-at-college-blame-sexism/.

14. "University of North Carolina at Chapel Hill," *College Navigator*, n.d., http://nces.ed.gov/collegenavigator/?q=university+of+north+carolina&s=all&id=199120.

15. School pass rates for licensure exams of other kinds can be hard to find. A given school may include them on a web page showing Student Right to Know or HEOA disclosures (Higher Education Opportunity Act of 2008, which amended the Higher Education Act of 1965). Northern Illinois University happens to be exemplary in this respect: See "Student Right to Know," *Northern Illinois University HEOA Disclosures*, n.d., http://www.niu.edu/disclosures/index.shtml. Otherwise, state governments publish pass rates in different forms.

16. Office of Communications, "Princeton Offers Admission to 6.46 Percent of Class of 2020," *Princeton University*, March 31, 2016, https://www.princeton.edu/main/news/archive/S45/94/44G37/index.xml?section=topstories; and "Application Dates & Deadlines," *Princeton University Undergraduate Admission*, 2016, https://admission.princeton.edu/applyingforadmission/application-dates-deadlines.

17. "Clemson University: Ranked among the Top 25 Public Universities in the Nation. U.S. News & World Report, 2016," *Clemson University*, n.d., https://www.clemson.edu/admissions/undergraduate/documents/breakfast-presentation.pdf.

18. Andrew Hacker and Claudia Dreifus, *Higher Education? How Colleges Are Wasting Our Money and Failing Our Kids and What We Can Do about It* (New York, NY: St. Martin's Press, 2010), 64–65.

19. "Admissions Statistics," *Harvard College, Office of Admissions & Financial Aid*, 2016, accessed September 9, 2016, https://college.harvard.edu/admissions/admissions-statistics.

20. "Our Selection Process: Applicant Profile," *Stanford University*, last updated July 25, 2016, accessed September 13, 2016, http://admission.stanford.edu/basics/selection/profile.html.

21. "Profile," *University of Virginia Office of Undergraduate Admission*, 2015, https://admission.virginia.edu/admission/profile; and "Student Profile," *TEXAS Admissions, The University of Texas at Austin*, n.d., https://admissions.utexas.edu/explore/freshman-profile.

22. Jon Levine, "9 Non-Ivy Colleges That Give Students a Better Bang for Their Buck than Harvard or Yale," *Mic*, April 27, 2015, http://mic.com/articles/116550/9-non-ivy-colleges-that-give-students-a-better-bang-for-their-buck-than-harvard-or-yale.

23. Frank Bruni, "A Prudent College Path," *New York Times*, August 8, 2015, http://www.nytimes.com/2015/08/09/opinion/sunday/frank-bruni-a-prudent-college-path.html?_r=0.

24. For the data, see "College Navigator," *National Center for Education Statistics*, n.d., https://nces.ed.gov/collegenavigator/.

25. "College Partnerships, and Articulation Agreements," *FinAid!*, n.d., http://www.finaid.org/otheraid/partnerships.phtml. As the article explains, outside of statewide mandates, there are articulation agreements. Articulation means matching community-college credits with requirements for a bachelor's degree. Articulation agreements are basically instruments made to smooth the path of transfer. Not all articulation agreements guarantee admission into public universities, nor are all such agreements results of statewide policy. Some are simply agreements between institutions. Serious savings are achievable, but cases vary, and interested parents need to look into the details of each case. The state of Massachusetts has also created an innovative program that gives 10 percent rebates for each successfully completed semester at a community college, upon a student's transfer to a four-year institution. Ashley A. Smith, "Rebate for Completion," *Inside Higher Ed*, April 22, 2016, https://www.insidehighered.com/news/2016/04/22/massachusetts-promotes-financial-rebates-incentivize-two-year-completion-and.

26. Scott Jaschik, "Princeton Will Resume Transfer Admissions," *Inside Higher Ed*, February 3, 2016, https://www.insidehighered.com/news/2016/02/03/princeton-university-will-resume-transfer-admissions-first-time-1990.

27. "90/10 Rule," *FinAid!*, n.d., http://www.finaid.org/loans/90-10-rule.phtml; and Chris Kirkham, "University of Phoenix Accreditation Hits Snag as Panel Recommends Probation," *Huffington Post*, February 25, 2013, accessed August 10, 2015, http://www.huffingtonpost.com/2013/02/25/university-of-phoenix-accreditation_n_2762168.html. Kirkham's reporting is based on a filing by the Apollo Group, which owns the University of Phoenix, with the Securities and Exchange Commission.

28. For a balanced account of the current state of for-profit higher education, see Ashley A. Smith, "Reshaping the For-Profit," *Inside Higher Ed*, July 15, 2015, https://www.insidehighered.com/news/2015/07/15/profit-industry-struggling-has-not-reached-end-road. Smith's main finding is that the industry has a future despite current negative publicity and new regulations. Experts predict that organizations will undergo reductions in size and further specialization but continue to be viable for-profit businesses.

29. Considerations for families interested in proprietary schools are listed in Robert Farrington, "Be Selective in Choosing a For-Profit College," *Forbes*, September 10, 2014, http://www.forbes.com/sites/robertfarrington/2014/09/10/be-selective-in-choosing-a-for-profit-college/.

30. Mark Phillips, "Why Should We Care about Vocational Education?," *Edutopia*, May 29, 2012, http://www.edutopia.org/blog/vocational-education-benefits-mark-phillips.

31. "Competency-Based Learning," *Western Governors University*, n.d., http://www.wgu.edu/why_WGU/competency_based_approach.

CHAPTER 3

1. Robert Morse and Eric Brooks, "Best Colleges Ranking Criteria and Weights," *U.S. News & World Report*, September 8, 2015, http://www.usnews.com/education/best-colleges/articles/ranking-criteria-and-weights.

2. "Memo RE: ACTA Survey Findings," *American Council of Trustees and Alumni with GfK Roper Public Affairs & Media*, August 2011, http://whatwillthey learn.com/public/pdfs/RoperFindings.pdf.

3. André Dua, *Voice of the Graduate* (New York, NY: McKinsey & Company in collaboration with Chegg, Inc., 2013), 8, 11, 13, http://mckinseyonsociety.com/down loads/reports/Education/UXC001%20Voice%20of%20the%20Graduate%20v7.pdf.

4. Brian Bourke, Nathaniel J. Bray, and C. Christopher Horton, "Approaches to the Core Curriculum: An Exploratory Analysis of Top Liberal Arts and Doctoral-Granting Institutions," *The Journal of General Education* 58, no. 4 (2009): 220.

5. Barry Latzer, *The Hollow Core: Failure of the General Education Curriculum* (Washington, DC: American Council of Trustees and Alumni, 2004), 2, http://files.eric.ed.gov/fulltext/ED535786.pdf.

6. Ibid.

7. Ibid., 2–3.

8. *National Assessment of Adult Literacy: A First Look at the Literacy of America's Adults in the 21st Century*, NCES 2006–470 (Jessup, MD: National Center for Education Statistics, 2006), 3–4, http://nces.ed.gov/NAAL/PDF/2006470.PDF; and Preety Sidhu and Valerie J. Calderon, "Many Business Leaders Doubt U.S. Colleges Prepare Students," *Gallup*, February 26, 2014, http://www.gallup.com/poll/167630/business-leaders-doubt-colleges-prepare-students.aspx.

9. *What Will They Learn? 2013–14* (Washington, DC: American Council of Trustees and Alumni, 2013), 1, https://www.goacta.org/images/download/what_will_they_learn_2013-14_report.pdf.

10. *What Will They Learn? 2016–17* (Washington, DC: American Council of Trustees and Alumni, 2016), 15–16, https://www.goacta.org/images/download/What_Will_They_Learn_2016-17.pdf.

11. "About the Major," *Amherst College*, n.d., https://www.amherst.edu/academiclife/departments/history/major.

12. "Requirements for the Major," *University of Wisconsin–Madison*, n.d., https://pubs.wisc.edu/ug/ls_history.htm#req.

13. Anne D. Neal, "Political Correctness and the Problems for Academic Freedom" (paper presented at the City Club of Cleveland, Cleveland, Ohio, October 3, 2014). The presentation excerpts KC Johnson, "The Assault on 'Traditional' U.S. History," (unpublished manuscript, 2010), 2.

14. *The Unkindest Cut: Shakespeare in Exile 2015* (Washington, DC: American Council of Trustees and Alumni, 2015), 3, https://www.goacta.org/images/download/ The_Unkindest_Cut.pdf.

15. William Faulkner, "Banquet Speech" (speech, Stockholm, Sweden, December 10, 1950), *Nobelprize.org*, http://www.nobelprize.org/nobel_prizes/literature/ laureates/1949/faulkner-speech.html.

16. Wage premiums for college graduates with STEM degrees far exceed premiums for college graduates with education and liberal arts degrees. (The premium is the difference between a college graduate's earnings and a high school graduate's.) See Anthony P. Carnevale and Ban Cheah, *From Hard Times to Better Times: College Majors, Unemployment, and Earnings* (Washington, DC: Center on Education and the Workforce, Georgetown University, 2015), https://cew.georgetown.edu/ wp-content/uploads/HardTimes2015-Report.pdf.

17. Jim Tankersley, "Starting College? Here's How to Graduate with a Job," *Washington Post Magazine*, August 9, 2013, https://www.washingtonpost.com/ lifestyle/magazine/starting-college-heres-how-to-graduate-with-a-job/2013/08/09/ 06805f36-ea79-11e2-a301-ea5a8116d211_story.html.

18. Meg P. Bernhard, "Class of 2019 by the Numbers: Harvard and Yale, in the Classroom and Out," (feature), *The Crimson*, n.d., http://features.thecrimson.com/ 2015/freshman-survey/academics-yale.

19. Tankersley, "Starting College? Here's How to Graduate with a Job."

20. Ralph Stinebrickner and Todd R. Stinebrickner, "A Major in Science? Initial Beliefs and Final Outcomes for College Major and Dropout," *Review of Economic Studies* 81, no. 1 (2014): 426–72.

21. Kevin Carey et al., "The University of Notre Dame: A Better Way of Teaching," *Choosing to Improve: Voices from Colleges and Universities with Better Graduation Rates* (Washington, DC: The Education Trust, 2005), 8, https://www.sdbor. edu/ad.

CHAPTER 4

1. Michael Poliakoff, "Bravo to Penn State," *American Council of Trustees and Alumni*, October 19, 2011, http://www.goacta.org/the_forum/bravo_to_penn_state.

2. Barry Strauss, "Donald Kagan Appreciation: The Scholar and Teacher" (presentation, 2005 Jefferson Lecturer, National Endowment for the Humanities, Washington, DC, 2005), http://www.neh.gov/about/awards/jefferson-lecture/donald-kagan-appreciation.

3. Eric Westervelt, "A Nobel Laureate's Education Plea: Revolutionize Teaching," *NPR*, April 14, 2016, http://www.npr.org/sections/ed/2016/04/14/ 465729968/a-nobel-laureates-education-plea-revolutionize-teaching.

4. Mark Bauerlein, "Professors on the Production Line, Students on Their Own" (working paper, American Enterprise Institute, 2009), 1–2; and Frederick M. Hess, "Foreward" in Bauerlein, "Professors on the Production Line, Students on Their Own," 1.

5. *Politics in the Classroom: A Survey of Students at the Top 50 Colleges & Universities* (Washington, DC: American Council of Trustees and Alumni, 2004), 2, 5, http://www.goacta.org/images/download/politics_in_the_classroom.pdf.

6. *Here We Have Idaho: A State Report Card on Public Higher Education* (Washington, DC: American Council of Trustees and Alumni with the Idaho Freedom Foundation, 2011), 11, http://www.goacta.org/images/download/here_we_have_idaho.pdf; *Show Me: A Report Card on Public Higher Education in Missouri* (Washington, DC: American Council of Trustees and Alumni, 2008), 10, http://www.goacta.org/images/download/show_me.pdf; Phyllis Palmiero, *Shining the Light: A Report Card on Georgia's System of Public Higher Education* (Washington, DC: American Council of Trustees and Alumni, 2008), 10, http://www.goacta.org/images/download/shining_the_light.pdf; *For the People: A Report Card on Public Higher Education in Illinois* (Washington, DC: American Council of Trustees and Alumni with the Illinois Policy Institute, 2009), 15, http://www.goacta.org/images/download/for_the_people.pdf; and *Made in Maine: A State Report Card on Public Higher Education* (Washington, DC: American Council of Trustees and Alumni with the Maine Heritage Policy Center, 2011), 13, http://mainepolicy.org/wp-content/uploads/Made-in-Maine-A-State-Report-Card-on-Higher-Education.pdf. Former Yale president Benno Schmidt and twenty-one other signatories say in the blue-chip report *Governance for a New Era* that "historically, there is evidence that self-interest and personal ideologies can drive departmental directions rather than the interest of the students and preparation of citizens." See Benno C. Schmidt, *Governance for a New Era: A Blueprint for Higher Education Trustees* (Washington, DC: American Council of Trustees and Alumni, 2014), 8, https://www.goacta.org/images/download/governance_for_a_new_era.pdf.

7. "The William F. Buckley, Jr. Program at Yale: Almost Half (49%) of U.S. College Students 'Intimidated' by Professors When Sharing Differing Beliefs: Survey," *McLaughlin & Associates*, October 26, 2015, http://mclaughlinonline.com/2015/10/26/the-william-f-buckley-jr-program-at-yale-almost-half-49-of-u-s-college-students-intimidated-by-professors-when-sharing-differing-beliefs-survey/.

8. David Koon, "T Is for Texas . . . and Transparency," *The James G. Martin Center for Academic Renewal*, October 30, 2009, http://www.popecenter.org/2009/10/t-is-for-texas-and-transparency/.

9. See http://explorer.opensyllabusproject.org/.

10. For more information about the American Council of Trustees and Alumni's directory of Oases of Excellence, visit http://www.goacta.org/initiatives/alumni_to_the_rescue_funding_oases_of_excellence.

11. Anne Neal, "Maximize Donor Value by Targeting Specific Programs," *Philanthropy Daily*, July 13, 2011, http://www.philanthropydaily.com/select-the-best/.

12. Ashley Thorne, "The I-Revel-in-My-Biases School of Social Work—And What It Does to a Student Who Declines to Join the Revelry," *National Association of Scholars*, February 21, 2008, https://www.nas.org/articles/The_I-Revel-in-My-Biases_School_of_Social_Work_--_And_What_It_Does_to_a_Stu.

13. George Will, "The Politically Correct Social Worker," *Long Beach Press-Telegram*, October 13, 2007, http://www.presstelegram.com/article/ZZ/20071013/NEWS/710139966.

CHAPTER 5

1. *Trouble in the Dorms: A Guide to Residential Life Programs for Higher Education Trustees* (Washington, DC: American Council of Trustees and Alumni, 2009), 3, https://www.goacta.org/images/download/trouble_in_the_dorms.pdf.

2. Ellen Tumposky, "Single-Sex Dorms Curb Binge Drinking and Hookups, College President Says," *ABC News*, June 16, 2011, http://abcnews.go.com/US/catholic-college-bucking-trend-returning-single-sex-dorms/story?id=13855333.

3. John Garvey, "Why We're Going Back to Single-Sex Dorms," *Wall Street Journal*, June 13, 2011, http://www.wsj.com/articles/SB10001424052702304432304576369843592242356.

4. Trish Wilson, "More College Campuses Are Offering Coed Dorm Rooms," *Philadelphia Inquirer*, May 18, 2010, http://articles.philly.com/2010-05-18/news/25217766_1_gender-neutral-gender-relations-dorm.

5. "UNC System Leaders Vote to Ban Gender-Neutral Housing," *WRAL.com*, last modified August 13, 2013, http://www.wral.com/unc-system-leaders-vote-to-ban-gender-neutral-housing/12758320/.

6. *Trouble in the Dorms*, 4–5.

7. Ibid.

8. "Residential Learning Communities," *University of Wisconsin–Madison*, n.d., https://www.housing.wisc.edu/residencehalls-lc.htm.

9. This text is no longer posted on the Green House page on the University of Wisconsin's website. It was quoted in an undated paper studying the University of Wisconsin's living-learning programming. See Aaron Brower, "Designing Effective Living-Learning Programs: Research and Praxis from the University of Wisconsin–Madison," *Association of American Colleges & Universities*, n.d., https://www.aacu.org/sites/default/files/Designing_Effective_LLPs.pdf.

10. "Witte Residence Hall," *University of Wisconsin–Madison*, n.d., https://www.housing.wisc.edu/residencehalls-halls-witte.htm.

11. "Welcome to Phillips Hall," *University of Wisconsin–Madison*, n.d., http://ssl1.linux.dwht.doit.wisc.edu/phillips.html. It is also illuminating that on another Wisconsin web page discussing this living-learning community, the following sentence appears: "Coming to college, you probably did not think that you would be watching Lady Gaga music videos for class [credit], but Open House makes that a reality." See "Open House: Gender Learning Community," *University of Wisconsin–Madison*, n.d., http://www.housing.wisc.edu/residencehalls-lc-openhouse.htm.

12. For a listing of different dorm positions, see "Dorm Life," *Bryn Mawr College,* n.d., http://www.brynmawr.edu/residentiallife/newstudents/dormlife.shtml.

13. Higher education scholar Gary Rhoades documents a crush of "managerial professionals" in "The Higher Education We Choose: A Question of Balance," *Review of Higher Education* 29, no. 3 (Spring 2006): 389–94.

14. See Benjamin Ginsberg, "Administrators Ate My Tuition," *Washington Monthly*, September/October 2011, http://www.washingtonmonthly.com/magazine/septemberoctober_2011/features/administrators_ate_my_tuition031641.php?page=all; Heather Mac Donald, "Harvard's Diversity Grovel," *City Journal*, June 3, 2005, http://www.city-journal.org/html/eon_06_03_05hm.html; Heather Mac Donald, "Less

Academics, More Narcissism," *City Journal*, July 14, 2011, http://www.city-journal.org/2011/cjc0714hm.html; and Adrianna Dinolfo, "1st Vice Chancellor for Equity and Inclusion Reflects on Time in Position," *The Daily Californian*, November 5, 2014, http://www.dailycal.org/2014/11/05/1st-vice-chancellor-equity-inclusion-reflects-time-position/. For example, the University of California–Berkeley's Division of Equity and Inclusion has grown from a staff of 3 to a staff of over 150.

15. "Student Conduct & Social Responsibility: Code of Student Conduct," Smith College, n.d., http://www.smith.edu/sao/handbook/socialconduct/socialcode.php.

16. *The Key: Student Handbook 2016–2017* (Hampden Sydney, VA: Hampden-Sydney College, 2016), 1, http://www.hsc.edu/Student-Life/The-Key-Student-Handbook/I-History-and-Traditions/Honor-and-Leadership.html.

17. Lisa W. Foderaro, "Without Cafeteria Trays, Colleges Find Savings," *New York Times*, April 28, 2009, http://www.nytimes.com/2009/04/29/nyregion/29tray.html.

18. Annie Massa, "Food for Thought: The Challenge of Healthy Eating on Campus," *USA TODAY College*, July 13, 2012, http://college.usatoday.com/2012/07/13/food-for-thought-the-challenge-of-healthy-eating-on-campus/.

19. Rachelle Peterson and Peter W. Wood, *Sustainability: Higher Education's New Fundamentalism* (New York, NY: National Association of Scholars, 2015), https://www.nas.org/images/documents/NAS-Sustainability-Digital.pdf.

20. Ibid., 11–12.

CHAPTER 6

1. *Substance Abuse on Campus: What Trustees Should Know* (Washington, DC: American Council of Trustees and Alumni, 2012), https://www.goacta.org/images/download/substance_abuse_on_campus.pdf.

2. These findings come from Ralph W. Hingson, Wenxing Zhu, and Elissa R. Weitzman, "Magnitude of and Trends in Alcohol-Related Mortality and Morbidity among U.S. College Students Ages 18–24, 1998–2005," *Journal of Studies on Alcohol and Drugs* Supplement no. 16 (July 2009): 12–20; and Ralph W. Hingson et al., "Magnitude of Alcohol-Related Mortality and Morbidity among U. S. College Students Ages 18–24," *Journal of Studies on Alcohol and Drugs* 63, no. 2 (2002): 141.

3. Tessa Berenson, "1 in 5: Debating the Most Controversial Sexual Assault Statistic," *TIME*, June 27, 2014, http://time.com/2934500/1-in-5%E2%80%82campus-sexual-assault-statistic/.

4. Shannon Luibrand, "Top Party Schools Named by the Princeton Review," *CBS News*, August 3, 2015, http://www.cbsnews.com/news/the-princeton-review-releases-list-of-top-party-schools-in-the-nation/.

5. Find the tool at http://ope.ed.gov/security/.

6. *Fostering Student Engagement Campuswide—Annual Results 2011* (Bloomington, IN: National Survey of Student Engagement, Indiana University Center for Postsecondary Research, 2011), 34, http://nsse.indiana.edu/nsse_2011_results/pdf/nsse_2011_annualresults.pdf; and "NSSE Annual Results 2015," *National Survey of Student Engagement, Indiana University Center for Postsecondary Research*, November 19, 2015, http://nsse.indiana.edu/html/annual_results.cfm.

7. Mary Beth Marklein, "College Freshmen Study Booze More than Books," *USA Today*, last modified March 11, 2009, http://usatoday30.usatoday.com/news/education/2009-03-11-college-drinking_N.htm; and *Substance Abuse on Campus: What Trustees Should Know*.

8. Stuart Rojstaczer and Christopher Healy, "Where A Is Ordinary: The Evolution of American College and University Grading, 1940–2009," *Teachers College Record* 114, no. 7 (2012): 1.

CHAPTER 7

1. Thomas Jefferson, *From Thomas Jefferson to William Roscoe, 27 December 1820*, letter, December 27, 1820, from National Archives, *Founders Online*, http://founders.archives.gov/documents/Jefferson/98-01-02-1712.

2. Edward R.A. Seligman et al., "1915 Declaration of Principles on Academic Freedom and Academic Tenure," *American Association of University Professors*, 1915, https://www.aaup.org/NR/rdonlyres/A6520A9D-0A9A-47B3-B550-C006B5B224E7/0/1915Declaration.pdf.

3. This quote originally appeared in Greg Lukianoff, *Unlearning Liberty: Campus Censorship and the End of American Debate* (New York, NY: Encounter Books, 2014). It was excerpted in Lukianoff's *Freedom from Speech* (New York, NY: Encounter Books, 2014), 7–8.

4. *Spotlight on Speech Codes 2016: The State of Free Speech on Our Nation's Campuses* (Philadelphia, PA: Foundation for Individual Rights in Education, 2016), 4, https://d28htnjz2elwuj.cloudfront.net/wp-content/uploads/2013/06/27212854/SCR_Final-Single_Pages.pdf. On FIRE's website, "school ratings" are organized under the category of "campus rights," as accessed on August 20, 2015. See https://www.thefire.org/spotlight/.

5. Samantha Harris, "Speech Code of the Month: Colby College," *Foundation for Individual Rights in Education*, July 20, 2016, https://www.thefire.org/speech-code-of-the-month-colby-college/.

6. "Colby College Harassment and Sexual Harassment Policy and Complaint Procedures," *Colby College*, last modified December 8, 2015, http://www.colby.edu/humanresources/wp-content/uploads/sites/170/2015/12/colby-college-harassment-and-sexual-harassment-policy-and-complaint-procedures.pdf; and Harris, "Speech Code of the Month: Colby College."

7. Anne D. Neal, "Political Correctness and the Problems for Academic Freedom" (paper presented at the City Club of Cleveland, Cleveland, Ohio, October 3, 2014).

8. Greg Lukianoff and Jonathan Haidt, "The Coddling of the American Mind," *The Atlantic*, September 2015, http://www.theatlantic.com/magazine/archive/2015/09/the-coddling-of-the-american-mind/399356/.

9. "A Resolution to Mandate Warnings for Triggering Content in Academic Settings," *Associated Students Senate, University of California, Santa Barbara*, February 25, 2014, https://www.as.ucsb.edu/senate/resolutions/a-resolution-to-mandate-warnings-for-triggering-content-in-academic-settings/; and Jenny Jarvie, "Trigger Happy," *New Republic*, March 4, 2014, https://newrepublic.com/article/116842/trigger-warnings-have-spread-blogs-college-classes-thats-bad.

10. See "Tool: Recognizing Microaggressions and the Messages They Send," in *Tools for Department Chairs and Deans* (Oakland, CA: University of California, Academic Personnel and Programs, n.d.), 3–4, https://diversity.ucsf.edu/sites/diversity.ucsf.edu/files/Tools%20for%20Department%20Chairs%20and%20Deans.pdf.

11. Katie Rogers, "Oberlin Students Take Culture War to the Dining Hall," *New York Times*, December 21, 2015, http://www.nytimes.com/2015/12/22/us/oberlin-takes-culture-war-to-the-dining-hall.html.

12. Scott D. Miller, "The Delicate Balance of Commencement," *Huffington Post*, May 29, 2014, http://www.huffingtonpost.com/dr-scott-d-miller/the-delicate-balance-of-c_b_5411059.html.

13. Richard Pérez-Peña and Tanzina Vega, "Brandeis Cancels Plan to Give Honorary Degree to Ayaan Hirsi Ali, a Critic of Islam," *New York Times*, April 8, 2014, http://www.nytimes.com/2014/04/09/us/brandeis-cancels-plan-to-give-honorary-degree-to-ayaan-hirsi-ali-a-critic-of-islam.html?_r=0.

14. Emma G. Fitzsimmons, "Condoleezza Rice Backs Out of Rutgers Speech after Student Protests," *New York Times*, May 3, 2014, http://www.nytimes.com/2014/05/04/nyregion/rice-backs-out-of-rutgers-speech-after-student-protests.html; and Maxwell Tani, "Obama Chides Rutgers Students for Pressuring Condoleeza Rice to Back Out of Commencement Speech," *Business Insider*, May 15, 2016, http://www.businessinsider.com/obama-rutgers-condolezza-rice-commencement-speech-2016-5.

15. Scott Jaschik, "Charles Murray Questions Azusa Pacific," *Inside Higher Ed*, April 23, 2014, https://www.insidehighered.com/quicktakes/2014/04/23/charles-murray-questions-azusa-pacific.

16. Mary Serreze, "Smith College Faculty Backlash Grows Following Christine Lagarde's Withdrawal as Commencement Speaker," *MassLive.com*, May 15, 2014, http://www.masslive.com/news/index.ssf/2014/05/smith_college_faculty_backlash.html.

17. C. Vann Woodward, "Report of the Committee to the Fellows of the Yale Corporation," in *Free to Teach, Free to Learn: Understanding and Maintaining Academic Freedom in Higher Education* (Washington, DC: American Council of Trustees and Alumni, 2013), 23–30, https://www.goacta.org/images/download/free_to_teach_free_to_learn.pdf.

CHAPTER 8

1. "Digest of Education Statistics: Table 326.10," *National Center for Education Statistics*, 2015, http://nces.ed.gov/programs/digest/d15/tables/dt15_326.10.asp?current=yes; and "Fast Facts," *National Center for Education Statistics*, 2016, https://nces.ed.gov/fastfacts/display.asp?id=40. The Beginning Postsecondary Students Longitudinal Study gives different national graduation rates, since it includes both first-time, full-time freshmen who graduate from the same institution, and students who transfer and receive a baccalaureate degree from another four-year institution. See Alexandria Walton Radford et al., *Persistence and Attainment of 2003–04 Beginning Postsecondary Students: After 6 Years* (Washington, DC:

National Center for Education Statistics, 2010), 11–12, Table 3, http://nces.ed.gov/pubs2011/2011151.pdf.

2. "Digest of Education Statistics: Table 326.10."

3. "Education Expenditures by Country," *National Center for Educational Statistics*, May 2016, http://nces.ed.gov/programs/coe/indicator_cmd.asp; and Liz Weston, "OECD: The U.S. Has Fallen behind Other Countries in College Completion," *Business Insider*, September 9, 2014, http://www.businessinsider.com/r-us-falls-behind-in-college-competition-oecd-2014-9.

4. "Freshman Retention Rate: National Universities," *U.S. News & World Report*, http://colleges.usnews.rankingsandreviews.com/best-colleges/rankings/national-universities/freshmen-least-most-likely-return; and Bill Destler, "Grade Inflation, Academic Rigor, and College Graduation Rates," *The Huffington Post*, December 9, 2014, http://www.huffingtonpost.com/bill-destler/grade-inflation-academic-_b_6278248.html.

5. Sara LaJeunesse, "Solving the Problem of Transferring Study-Abroad Credits," *Penn State College of Education*, February 2012, https://ed.psu.edu/news/news-items-jan-mar-2012/solving-the-problem-of-transferring-study-abroad-credits.html.

6. "Selecting a College—Engagement Matters: A College Planning Checklist," *Purdue University*, n.d., http://www.purdue.edu/checklist/.

7. Ibid.

8. Gabrielle Russon, "More College Students Paying Double for Excess Credit Hours," *Orlando Sentinel*, May 22, 2016, http://www.orlandosentinel.com/features/education/os-credit-hour-surcharge-20160522-story.html. The surcharge applies only if students exceed the credit requirement by more than 10 percent.

CHAPTER 9

1. In 2013, average sum of tuition and required fees at postsecondary institutions was $10,683, and the median household income was $52,250. See "Digest of Education Statistics: Table 330.10," *National Center for Education Statistics*, 2013, https://nces.ed.gov/programs/digest/d13/tables/dt13_330.10.asp; and Amanda Noss, "Household Income: 2013," *American Community Survey Briefs*, ACSBR/13–02 (Washington, DC: United States Census Bureau, 2014), 3, Table 1, https://www.census.gov/content/dam/Census/library/publications/2014/acs/acsbr13-02.pdf.

2. Meta Brown et al., "The Student Loan Landscape," *Federal Reserve Bank of New York*, February 18, 2015, http://libertystreeteconomics.newyorkfed.org/2015/02/the_student_loan-landscape.html. See the chart entitled "Distribution of Student Loan Borrowers by Balance in 2014."

3. Donghoon Lee, "Household Debt and Credit: Student Debt" (slide presentation, Federal Reserve Bank of New York, New York, NY, February 28, 2013), accessed August 24, 2015, https://www.newyorkfed.org/medialibrary/media/news events/mediaadvisory/2013/Lee022813.pdf; and Josh Mitchell, "School-Loan Reckoning: 7 Million Are in Default," *Wall Street Journal*, last modified August 21, 2015,

http://www.wsj.com/articles/about-7-million-americans-havent-paid-federal-student-loans-in-at-least-a-year-1440175645. Delinquency is defined as having failed to make a payment of their student debt for more than 90 days past the deadline, while default is defined as having failed to make a payment for more than 360 days.

4. "Tuition and Fees and Room and Board over Time, 1975–76 to 2015–16, Selected Years," in *Trends in Higher Education, College Board*, n.d., https://trends.collegeboard.org/college-pricing/figures-tables/tuition-and-fees-and-room-and-board-over-time-1975-76-2015-16-selected-years. Between 1975–1976 and 2015–2016, the total cost of tuition and required fees at private, not-for-profit four-year colleges more than tripled, while the total cost at public colleges nearly quadrupled.

5. Sandy Baum and Jennifer Ma, *Trends in College Pricing 2014* in *Trends in Higher Education* series (n.p.: College Board, 2014), 26, Table 15A, http://trends.collegeboard.org/sites/default/files/2014-trends-college-pricing-final-web.pdf. In 2011–2012, families in the "lowest income quartile" were offered a discount of 56 percent of total published expenses at institutions in the "highest tuition group" of private, not-for-profit four-year schools. See also Jeffrey J. Selingo, *College (Un)bound: The Future of Higher Education and What It Means for Students* (New York, NY: Houghton Mifflin Harcourt, 2013), 29. Selingo finds that "the *average* discount for first-year students at private colleges is now a staggering 42 percent."

6. David Radwin et al., *2011–12 National Postsecondary Student Aid Study*, NCES 2013–165 (Washington, DC: National Center for Education Statistics, 2013), 7, Table 1, http://nces.ed.gov/pubs2013/2013165.pdf. Around 70.7 percent of students will receive some form of aid, and 59.1 percent receive grants to defray their cost of education.

7. An explication of this mandate intended for compliance purposes is given in David A. Bergeron, "Subject: Guidance on Implementing the Net Price Calculator Requirement," *US Department of Education*, February 27, 2013, accessed August 22, 2015, http://ifap.ed.gov/dpcletters/GEN1307.html.

8. Beckie Supiano, "A Low-Cost Way to Expand the Horizons of High-Achieving, Low-Income Students," *Chronicle of Higher Education*, March 29, 2013, http://chronicle.com/article/A-Low-Cost-Way-to-Expand-the/138227/; and Caroline M. Hoxby and Christopher Avery, "The Missing 'One-Offs': The Hidden Supply of High-Achieving, Low-Income Students," *Brookings Papers on Economic Activity* (Spring 2013): 1–50.

9. Mark Kantrowitz, "Colleges with 'No Loans' Financial Aid Policies," *Edvisors*, n.d., accessed August 24, 2015, https://www.edvisors.com/plan-for-college/money-saving-tips/no-loans-colleges/; and Akane Otani, "Ten Elite Schools Where Middle-Class Kids Don't Pay Tuition," *Bloomberg*, April 1, 2015, http://www.bloomberg.com/news/articles/2015-04-01/ten-elite-schools-where-middle-class-kids-don-t-pay-tuition. Some schools apply no-loans policies to all students, while others apply them for students from low-income families specifically.

10. Ry Rivard, "Summer Scramble," *Inside Higher Ed*, May 21, 2014, https://www.insidehighered.com/news/2014/05/21/colleges-miss-enrollment-targets-step-their-summer-recruitment. Schools are often willing to use financial aid as a carrot to attract prospective students and meet enrollment targets.

11. See Selingo, supra note 144. He gives 42 percent as the cautious estimate of the average discount given to incoming students at private colleges.

12. *Four-Year Myth* (Indianapolis, IN: Complete College America, 2014), 4, http://completecollege.org/wp-content/uploads/2014/11/4-Year-Myth.pdf.

13. "Should Your College Be Public or Private?" *COLLEGEdata*, n.d., http://www.collegedata.com/cs/content/content_choosearticle_tmpl.jhtml?articleId=10008.

14. Katy Hopkins, "More Schools Debut Tuition Guarantee Plans," *U.S. News & World Report*, February 22, 2012, http://www.usnews.com/education/best-colleges/paying-for-college/articles/2012/02/22/more-schools-debut-tuition-guarantee-programs.

15. Annamaria Andriotis, "Fewer Parents Are Saving for College," *Wall Street Journal*, April 29, 2015, http://blogs.wsj.com/totalreturn/2015/04/29/fewer-parents-are-saving-for-college/.

16. To view commonly asked questions about the FAFSA, visit "FAFSA Help," *Office of Federal Student Aid, U.S. Department of Education*, n.d., https://fafsa.ed.gov/help.htm. See the FAFSA form here: https://www.edvisors.com/media/files/fafsa-forms/current-year-fafsa-form-english.pdf.

17. Edvisors finds that "more than 95 percent (95.9%) of Federal Pell Grant recipients in 2011–12 had family adjusted gross income (AGI) under $60,000" in "Federal Pell Grant," *Edvisors*, n.d., accessed September 2, 2015, https://www.edvisors.com/scholarships/grants/federal-pell-grant/.

18. *Funding Your Education: The Guide to Federal Student Aid* (Washington, DC: U.S. Department of Education, 2014), 4, https://studentaid.ed.gov/sa/sites/default/files/funding-your-education.pdf.

19. "Disbursing Pell Awards" in *Volume 3. Pell Grants, 2003–2004* (Washington, DC: Information for Financial Aid Professionals, U.S. Department of Education, 2003), https://ifap.ed.gov/sfahandbooks/attachments/0304Vol3Ch4.pdf.

20. *Publication 970: Tax Benefits for Education* (Washington, DC: Internal Revenue Service, 2016), http://www.irs.gov/pub/irs-pdf/p970.pdf.

21. Federal Reserve Bank of New York, "Household Debt Continues Upward Climb while Student Loan Delinquencies Worsen," press release, February 17, 2015, https://www.newyorkfed.org/newsevents/news/research/2015/rp150217.html.

22. "Subsidized and Unsubsidized Loans," *Federal Student Aid, An Office of the U.S. Department of Education*, n.d., https://studentaid.ed.gov/sa/types/loans/subsidized-unsubsidized#subsidized-vs-unsubsidized.

23. "Nursing Student Loans," *Health Resources and Services Administration*, n.d., http://www.hrsa.gov/loanscholarships/loans/nursing.html. Nursing loans are a program of the U.S. Department of Health and Human Services.

24. "PLUS Loans," *Federal Student Aid, An Office of the U.S. Department of Education*, n.d., https://studentaid.ed.gov/sa/types/loans/plus#eligibility.

25. "Perkins Loans," *Federal Student Aid, An Office of the U.S. Department of Education*, n.d., https://studentaid.ed.gov/sa/types/loans/perkins.

26. Peterson's Staff, "Federal Student Aid and Work-Study Awards," *Peterson's*, July 27, 2016, https://www.petersons.com/college-search/student-aid-work-study.aspx. For more on federal aid, visit the website of the U.S. Department of Education's Office of Federal Student Aid, https://studentaid.ed.gov/sa/.

27. Sandy Baum et al., *Trends in Student Aid 2015* in *Trends in Higher Education* series (n.p.: College Board, 2015), Figure 2013_9B, http://trends.collegeboard.org/

student-aid/figures-tables/percentage-undergraduate-and-graduate-students-borrowing-private-loans-over-time.

28. "Federal versus Private Loans," *Federal Student Aid, An Office of the U.S. Department of Education*, n.d., https://studentaid.ed.gov/sa/types/loans/federal-vs-private.

29. Beth Akers, "How Income Share Agreements Could Play a Role in Higher Ed Financing," *Brookings Institution*, October 16, 2014, https://www.brookings.edu/research/how-income-share-agreements-could-play-a-role-in-higher-ed-financing/.

30. Danielle Douglas-Gabriel, "The Obama Administration's Plan to Lower the Student Debt Payments of Millions More Americans," *Get There* (blog), *Washington Post*, July 10, 2015, https://www.washingtonpost.com/news/get-there/wp/2015/07/10/the-obama-administrations-plan-to-lower-the-student-debt-payments-of-millions-more-americans/.

31. "529 Plan Comparison by Plan Name," *College Savings Plans Network*, n.d., http://plans.collegesavings.org/planComparisonState.aspx; and "Did You Know?", *College Savings Plans Network*, n.d., http://www.collegesavings.org/did-you-know/.

32. "My Tax Adviser Is Recommending 529 Plans as an Estate-Planning Vehicle. What Is the Advantage?" *Savingforcollege.com*, n.d., http://www.savingforcollege.com/grandparents/answer.php?grandparent_faq_id=11. Grandparents may contribute up to $14,000 each year while retaining tax exemption on the sum.

33. See College Scorecard (collegescorecard.ed.gov) for more school-level data about debt.

34. See Mark Kantrowitz's quote in Stephen Pounds, "How to Avoid the Stranglehold of Too Much Student Loan Debt," *Bankrate*, http://www.bankrate.com/finance/college-finance/how-much-college-debt-is-too-much-1.aspx; Susie Poppick, "Here's What the Average Grad Makes Right Out of College," *Money*, April 22, 2015, http://time.com/money/3829776/heres-what-the-average-grad-makes-right-out-of-college/; and Emily Peck, "The Class of 2015 Is in for a Rude Awakening on Pay," *Huffington Post*, May 12, 2015, http://www.huffingtonpost.com/2015/05/12/college-grad-starting-salary_n_7265090.html. Some students could make more, depending on their major, and survey results of average earnings vary dramatically.

35. Peck, "The Class of 2015 Is in for a Rude Awakening on Pay."

36. Adam Davidson, "It's Official: The Boomerang Kids Won't Leave," *New York Times*, June 20, 2014, http://www.nytimes.com/2014/06/22/magazine/its-official-the-boomerang-kids-wont-leave.html.

37. Janet Lorin, "Parents Snared in $100 Billion College Debt Trap Risk Retirement," *Bloomberg*, February 2, 2012, http://www.bloomberg.com/news/articles/2012-02-02/parents-snared-in-100-billion-u-s-college-debt-trap-risking-retirement.

38. "Parent PLUS Loan Overview," *Edvisors*, n.d., https://www.edvisors.com/college-loans/federal/parent-plus/introduction-to-federal-parent-plus-loans/; for more, see "Parent PLUS Loans vs. Private Student Loans," *Edvisors*, n.d., https://www.edvisors.com/college-loans/federal/parent-plus/compare/. The 6.31 percent rate is set for the 2016–2017 academic year.

39. Tyler Kingkade, "Martin O'Malley Calls for Debt-Free College within 5 Years," *Huffington Post*, July 7, 2015, http://www.huffingtonpost.com/2015/07/07/omalley-debt-free-college_n_7748504.html.

CHAPTER 10

1. "Core Curriculum," *Columbia Undergraduate Admissions*, n.d., https://under grad.admissions.columbia.edu/learn/academiclife/college/core.

2. "Finding Textbooks at the University of Pennsylvania: Where to Buy Course Texts," *Penn Libraries, University of Pennsylvania*, last modified August 4, 2016, http://guides.library.upenn.edu/c.php?g=475175&p=3254093.

3. "The Edge Career Center," Randolph-Macon College, n.d., http://www.rmc.edu/prospective-students/randolph-macon-edge; and "The Edge Career Boot Camp: Hands-on Career Training," *Randolph-Macon College*, January 6, 2015, http://www.rmc.edu/news-and-calendar/current-news/2015/01/06/the-edge-career-boot-camp-hands-on-career-training.

4. Mark Schneider, *Higher Education Pays: But a Lot More for Some Graduates than for Others* (Rockville, MD: College Measures' Economic Success Metrics Project, 2013), 2, http://www.air.org/sites/default/files/Higher_Education_Pays_Sep_13.pdf.

CHAPTER 11

1. *What Will They Learn? 2014–15: A Survey of Core Requirements at Our Nation's Colleges and Universities* (Washington, DC: American Council of Trustees and Alumni, 2014), https://www.goacta.org/images/download/what_will_they_learn_2014-15_report.pdf.

2. "Structure of the U.S. Education System: Credit Systems," *International Affairs Office, U.S. Department of Education*, February 2008, https://www2.ed.gov/about/offices/list/ous/international/usnei/us/credits.doc.

3. Nate Johnson, Leonard Reidy, Mike Droll, and R. E. LeMon, *Program Requirements for Associate's and Bachelor's Degrees: A National Survey* (Washington, DC: Complete College America, 2012), 2, http://completecollege.org/docs/Program%20 Requirements%20-%20A%20National%20Survey.pdf.

4. Susannah Snider, "Know Your Risk Factors for Delaying Graduation, Accumulating More Debt," *U.S. News & World Report*, September 23, 2014, http://www.usnews.com/education/best-colleges/paying-for-college/articles/2014/09/23/know-your-risk-factors-for-delaying-graduation-accumulating-more-debt; and Matthew J. Foraker, *Does Changing Majors Really Affect the Time to Graduate? The Impact of Changing Majors on Student Retention, Graduation, and Time to Graduate* (Bowling Green, KY: Office of Institutional Research, Western Kentucky University, 2012), https://www.wku.edu/instres/documents/air_major_change.pdf.

5. Kathy Boccella, "Diversity Program Creates Division: Delaware Freshmen Unsettled," *Philadelphia Inquirer*, November 2, 2007, http://articles.philly.com/2007-11-02/news/25225331_1_diversity-training-program-students-resident-advisers.

6. Robert Shibley, "A Warning to College Parents and Grandparents," *Daily Caller*, August 11, 2011, http://dailycaller.com/2011/08/11/a-warning-to-college-parents-and-grandparents/2/.

7. See the Stand Up for Speech Litigation Project's website, http://www.standup forspeech.com/.

8. George Leef, "Sustainability: A New College Fad with Fangs," *John William Pope Center for Higher Education Policy*, April 15, 2015, http://www.popecenter. org/2015/04/sustainability-a-new-college-fad-with-fangs/.

9. Stephanie B. Garlock and Hana N. Rouse, "Harvard College Introduces Pledge for Freshmen to Affirm Values," *Harvard Crimson*, September 1, 2011, http://www.thecrimson.com/article/2011/9/1/pledge-freshmen-students-harvard/.

10. For a thoughtful statement of reasons to oppose this measure, see Harry Lewis, "The Freshman Pledge," *Bits and Pieces* (blog), August 30, 2011, http://harry-lewis.blogspot.com/2011/08/freshman-pledge.html. See also Max Brindle, "As Goes Harvard . . . ," *The Forum: A Town Square for Higher Ed* (blog), *American Council of Trustees and Alumni*, August 31, 2011, http://www.goacta.org/the_forum/as_goes_harvard; and Harvey Silverglate and Juliana DeVries, "Harvard, Where Civility Trumps Free Speech," *Minding the Campus*, September 23, 2012, http://www.mindingthecampus.org/2012/09/_harvard_where_civility_trumps/.

11. "Bachelor's Degrees in the Humanities," *American Academy of Arts and Sciences*, March 2016, Chart II-1b, http://humanitiesindicators.org/content/indicatordoc. aspx?i=34.

12. Scott Jaschik, "Kentucky's Governor vs. French Literature," *Inside Higher Ed*, February 1, 2016, https://www.insidehighered.com/quicktakes/2016/02/01/kentuckys-governor-vs-french-literature.

13. John Henry Newman, *The Idea of a University* (London and New York, NY: Longman, Green, 1899; and New Haven, CT: Yale University Press, 1996), discourse 7, section 9.

14. Newman, *The Idea of a University*, discourse 9, section 8.

15. The quote appears in Robert E. Beck, *Career Patterns: The Liberal Arts Major in Bell System Management* (Washington, DC: Association of American Colleges, 1981), 13.

16. Hart Research Associates, *It Takes More than a Major: Employer Priorities for College Learning and Student Success* (Washington, DC: Hart Research Associates, 2013), 1, http://www.aacu.org/leap/documents/2013_EmployerSurvey.pdf.

17. Casner-Lotto, Jill et al., *Are They Really Ready to Work? Employers' Perspectives on the Basic Knowledge and Applied Skills of New Entrants to the 21st Century U.S. Workforce* (New York, NY: The Conference Board, 2006), http://www. p21.org/storage/documents/FINAL_REPORT_PDF09-29-06.pdf.

18. Scott Jaschik, "'Academically Adrift,'" *Inside Higher Ed*, January 18, 2011, https://www.insidehighered.com/news/2011/01/18/study_finds_large_numbers_of_college_students_don_t_learn_much.

19. Richard Arum, et al., *Documenting Uncertain Times: Post-Graduate Transitions of the* Academically Adrift *Cohort* (New York, NY: Social Science Research Council, 2012), 3–4, https://s3.amazonaws.com/ssrc-cdn1/crmuploads/new_publication_3/%7BFCFB0E86-B346-E111-B2A8-001CC477EC84%7D.pdf.

20. Bureau of Labor Statistics, "Number of Jobs Held, Labor Market Activity, and Earnings Growth among the Youngest Baby Boomers: Results from a Longitudinal Survey," press release, March 31, 2015, http://www.bls.gov/news.release/pdf/nlsoy.pdf.

21. Jim Tankersley, "Starting College? Here's How to Graduate with a Job," *Washington Post*, August 9, 2013, https://www.washingtonpost.com/lifestyle/magazine/starting-college-heres-how-to-graduate-with-a-job/2013/08/09/06805f36-ea79-11e2-a301-ea5a8116d211_story.html.

22. Information about FERPA is posted by the Department of Education's Family Compliance Office at http://familypolicy.ed.gov/?src=fpco-faqs and http://family policy.ed.gov/faq-page.

23. Robert Turrisi et al., "Evaluation of Timing and Dosage of a Parent Based Intervention to Minimize College Students' Alcohol Consumption," *Journal of Studies on Alcohol and Drugs* 74, no. 1 (January 2013): 30–40, http://www.ncbi.nlm.nih.gov/pubmed/?term=PMC3517262.

24. See Susan Feinstein, "Will You Be Able to Help Your College Age Child in a Medical Emergency?", *Consumer Reports*, July 23, 2016, http://www.consumer reports.org/cro/news/2014/08/will-you-be-able-to-help-your-college-age-child-in-a-health-emergency/index.htm.

CHAPTER 12

1. Thomas Jefferson, "Extract from Thomas Jefferson to Charles Yancey," *Thomas Jefferson Foundation*, written January 6, 1816, http://tjrs.monticello.org/letter/327.

2. Gene Zechmeister, "Timeline of the Founding of the University of Virginia," *Thomas Jefferson Foundation*, July 5, 2011, https://www.monticello.org/site/research-and-collections/timeline-founding-university-virginia; and "About Hampden-Sydney College," *Hampden-Sydney College*, n.d., http://www.hsc.edu/About-H-SC.html.

3. "Alexander Hamilton," *Columbia 250*, 2004, http://c250.columbia.edu/c250_celebrates/remarkable_columbians/alexander_hamilton.html.

4. "Penn's Heritage," *University of Pennsylvania*, n.d., http://www.upenn.edu/about/history.

5. "Our Namesakes," *Washington and Lee University*, n.d., https://www.wlu.edu/about-wandl/history-and-traditions/our-namesakes.

POSTSCRIPT: TAKE ACTION

1. *Higher Educational Institutions; Restrictions on Student Speech, Limitations*, HB 258, Virginia's Legislative Information System, April 4, 2014, https://lis.virginia.gov/cgi-bin/legp604.exe?141+sum+HB258.

APPENDIX A

1. Adapted by permission from a letter dated February 27, 2014, by Greg Lewin and published in *Inside Academe*, May, 2014, when Mr. Lewin was an employee of the American Council of Trustees and Alumni. Mr. Lewin received a BA from George Washington University in 2012 and an MA from the Hubert H. Humphrey School of Public Affairs, University of Minnesota, in 2016.

About the Author

Anne D. Neal is co-founder of the American Council of Trustees and Alumni and was its president from 2003 to 2016. She currently serves as senior fellow. She is a graduate of Harvard College and Harvard Law School.